# THE ART OF CONVERSATION

# THE ART OF
# CONVERSATION

PETER BURKE

Cornell University Press
Ithaca, New York

First published 1993 by Cornell University Press.


Library of Congress Cataloging-in-Publication Data

Burke, Peter
    The art of conversation / Peter Burke.
        p.    cm.
    Includes bibliographical references (p.) and index.
    ISBN 0–8014–2956–0.—ISBN 0–8014–8167–8
    1. Conversation.    2. Oral communication—Europe—History.
    I. Title.
    P95.45.B87    1993
    302.3′46—dc20                                                                   93–10831


This book is printed on acid-free paper.

Printed in Great Britain.

# Contents

# Preface

Although learning languages has long been a hobby of mine, it was only in the late 1970s that I began to read the sociolinguists and to think seriously about the problems of incorporating language into social and cultural history. I soon discovered that other British historians were thinking on similar lines – Raphael Samuel, for instance, Gareth Stedman Jones, and Jonathan Steinberg. Discussions with them and conferences in Dublin, Cambridge and Brighton helped me to formulate these problems more precisely, and to reflect on possible methods of approaching them. Working with Ruth Finnegan on the series of Cambridge Studies in Oral and Literate Culture increased my awareness of the variety of oral styles. Most important of all has been the dialogue with Roy Porter in the course of our editing two volumes of essays on the social history of language (not to mention planning a third).

Written originally as conference or seminar papers, these essays are deliberately exploratory rather than definitive, an attempt to reconnoitre terrain which the next generation may well cultivate more intensively. I have taken advantage of the opportunity afforded by this collected edition to revise or develop the argument in some places, to add more examples, and to take account of recent work in both history and linguistics, as well as eliminating repetitions and making the system of references uniform.

I am grateful to Cambridge University Press for permission to reprint chapter 1, and to the Center for Kulturforskning, Aarhus University, for permission to reprint chapter 3. The essay on silence will be delivered as my 'farewell lecture' at the University of Nijmegen in 1993 and published by the university press there, while the essay on conversation appears in print for the first time.

The international Republic of Letters, more effective than ever in the age of jets and word processors, has been extremely supportive of this project. I have learned a good deal from the discussions following talks on these themes in different parts of the world (including the polyglot environments of Helsinki and Vienna). I am especially grateful to Rudolf Dekker for the information – on Dutch, on Latin, on silence – which he has sent me over the years. Chapter 2 in particular has benefited from the advice and the references offered by an international group of scholars, including Rino Avesani, Derek Beales, Dietrich Briesemeister, Zweder von Martels, Robert Muchembled, Eva Österberg, Roy Porter, Nigel Spivey, and Joe Trapp. I am most grateful to them all. My wife, Maria Lúcia Pallares-Burke, read the draft chapters with a critical eye and drew my attention to some eighteenth-century texts. She has also initiated me into life in a bilingual environment. The book is dedicated to her.

# 1

# The Social History of Language

In the last few years a relatively new area of historical research has developed, which might be described as a social history of language, a social history of speaking, or a social history of communication. Consciousness of the importance of language in everyday life has become widespread in the last generation or so. As the rise of feminist and regionalist movements shows, dominated groups have become more sharply aware of the power of language as well as the involvement of language with other forms of power. Again, the philosophers, critics and others associated with the movements commonly labelled structuralism and deconstruction, despite their many disagreements, share a strong concern with language and its place in culture.

Whether they are involved with one or more of these movements, or with oral history, another recent development, a number of historians have also come to recognize the need for the study of language for two reasons in particular. In the first place, as an end in itself, as a social institution, as a part of culture and everyday life. In the second place, as a means to the better understanding of oral and written sources via awareness of their linguistic conventions.[1] All the same, there still remains a

[1] Recent collections of essays along these lines include Burke and Porter (1987, 1991) and Corfield (1991). Earlier examples of work by historians include Armstrong (1965); Béranger (1969); Brosnahan (1963); Macmullen (1962); Richter (1975, 1979); Bertelli (1976); as well as the pioneers cited in note 23.

gap between the disciplines of history, linguistics, and sociology (including social anthropology). The gap can and should be filled by a social history of language.

It is no new idea that language has a history. Ancient Romans, such as Varro, and Renaissance humanists, such as Leonardo Bruni and Flavio Biondo, were interested in the history of Latin.[2] Discussions of the origin of French, Italian, Spanish, and other languages were published in the sixteenth and seventeenth centuries, forming part of the debates about the relative merits of Latin and the vernaculars and the correct ways of speaking and writing the latter.[3]

In the nineteenth century, the dominant school of linguists, the so-called 'neogrammarians', was much concerned with the reconstruction of early forms of particular languages, such as 'protoromance' and 'protogermanic', and with the formulation of laws of linguist evolution.[4] This was the approach against which the linguistic Ferdinand de Saussure, now seen as the father of structuralism, reacted, on the grounds that the historical school of linguists was too little concerned with the relation between the different parts of the language system.[5] In Saussure's day, however, the historical approach remained dominant. The Oxford English Dictionary, planned, as its title-page declared, on 'historical principles', began publication in 1884, while its French equivalent, edited by Emile Littré, began in 1863.[6] Histories of English, French and German which have since achieved the status of classics date originally from the years around 1900.[7]

All the same, this approach to the history of language lacked a full social dimension. Children of their time, these nineteenth-century scholars thought of language as an organism which 'grows' or 'evolves' through definite stages and expresses the values or 'spirit' of the nation which speaks it. Their concerns were national — or even nationalist — rather than social. They studied the internal history of languages, the history of their structure, but neglected what has been called their 'external his-

[2]   Klein (1957).
[3]   Bembo (1525); Pasquier (1566); Cittadini (1604); Aldrete (1606).
[4]   Aarsleff (1967); Bynon (1977), ch.1; Crowley (1989), 13–50.
[5]   Culler (1976), esp. ch. 3; Corfield (1991).
[6]   Crowley (1989).
[7]   Behaghel (1898); Jespersen (1905); Brunot (1905–).

tory', in other words the history of their use.[8] They showed little interest in the different varieties of the 'same' language spoken by different social groups. On the other hand, this concern is central to contemporary sociolinguistics, which crystallized into a discipline in the late 1950s in the United States and elsewhere.

Of course, awareness of the social significance of varieties of speech is far from new. It has been argued with some plausibility that in Italy the sixteenth century was 'the time in which language first came to be regarded as a primarily social phenomenon'.[9] One Italian writer published a book in 1547 'On Speech and Silence', organizing the study according to the modern-sounding categories 'who', 'to whom', 'why', 'how', and 'when',[10] thus reminding us of the debt which sociolinguistics owes to the tradition of classical rhetoric.

Other writers also made acute sociolinguistic observations at this time. Vincenzo Borghini, for example, noted and tried to explain the archaism of the speech of Tuscan peasants, arguing that 'they converse less with foreigners than townspeople do, and for this reason change less.' In his famous dialogue on 'civil conversation', Stefano Guazzo described the harsh accent of the Piedmontese, the Genoese propensity to swallow their words, the Florentines with their mouths 'full of aspirations', and so on.[11]

A similar sociolinguistic awareness can be found in the plays of Shakespeare. In a famous scene in *Henry IV*, for example, Hotspur criticizes his Kate for saying 'in good sooth' because this turn of phrase was not aristocratic. 'You swear like a comfit-maker's wife,' he tells her. What Hotspur wanted to hear was 'a good mouth-filling oath'. In the seventeenth century, Molière, as we shall see below, had his ear particularly well tuned to the social nuances expressed by different varieties of language. One might say the same of Goldoni in the following century.

Nineteenth-century novels, from Jane Austen and George Eliot to Leo Tolstoy and Theodor Fontane, are a still richer source of observations on the social meaning of differences in speech. Think, for example, of Rosamond Vincy in *Middlemarch*, objecting

[8] Hall (1974).
[9] Hall (1942), 54.
[10] Politiano (1547).
[11] Borghini (1971), 139; Guazzo (1574), 79.

to her mother's phrase 'the pick of them' as 'rather a vulgar expression', while her carefree brother Fred counters with the assertion – which has its parallel among linguists today – that so-called 'correct' English is nothing but 'the slang of prigs'. When the old lawyer Standish, in the same novel, swears 'By God!', the author intervens to explain that he was using that oath as 'a sort of armorial bearings, stamping the speech of a man who held a good position'. He used it, as we might say, as a status symbol.[12]

The perceptiveness and articulateness of these writers was out of the ordinary. All the same, there would be little need for a social history of language if ordinary speakers were not more or less aware of the social meaning of styles of speech, while social climbers have always been hyperconscious of such matters.

Again, it is no new idea that language is a potential instrument in the hands of the ruling class, an instrument which they may employ as much to mystify or to control as to communicate. The use of Latin in early modern Europe is an obvious example, and it will be discussed in detail below (p. 37). The use of another foreign language, 'law French', in English courts was criticized on similar grounds by men as diverse as Archbishop Thomas Cranmer, King James I, and the seventeenth-century radicals John Lilburne and John Warr.[13] Again, in the middle of the nineteenth century, the British sociologist Herbert Spencer was already recommending historical research on what he called 'the control exercised by class over class, as displayed in social observances – in titles, salutations and forms of address'.[14]

All the same, as the philosopher Alfred Whitehead once remarked, 'Everything of importance has been said before by someone who did not discover it.' In other words, there is an enormous difference between the vague awareness of a problem and systematic research into it. In the case of the relation between language, thought and society, pioneering explorations were made from the end of the nineteenth century onwards, notably by the sociologist Thorstein Veblen, the literary critic Mikhail Bakhtin, and the linguists Fritz Mauthner, Benjamin Whorf and Antoine Meillet.

Veblen, for example, paid serious attention to linguistic

[12] On English novelists, Phillipps (1984), *passim.*
[13] Hill (1972), 269–76.
[14] Spencer (1861), 26.

phenomena when formulating his famous 'theory of the leisure class'.[15] Bakhtin criticized the structural linguist Saussure for his lack of interest in change over time and developed the theory of 'heteroglossia' (*raznorechie*) according to which a language, Russian for instance, is the result of the interplay or struggle between different dialects, jargons and so on, different forms of language which are associated with different social groups and their diverse points of view, so that each user of language has to appropriate it from the mouths of others and adapt it to his or her own needs.[16]

Fritz Mauthner by contrast was a linguistic determinist. Developing Nietzsche's idea of language as a 'prison' (*Gefängnis*), Mauthner once declared that 'if Aristotle had spoken Chinese or Dakotan, he would have produced a totally different system of logical categories' ('Hätte Aristoteles Chinesisch oder Dakotaisch gesprochen, er hätte zu einer qanz andern Logik gelangen müssen').[17] Whorf's controversial but influential essays made essentially the same point, arguing that the fundamental ideas of a people, such as the Hopi Indians – their conceptions of time, space, and so on – are shaped by the structure of their language, its genders, tenses, and other grammatical and syntactical forms.[18]

In France, Antoine Meillet, a former pupil of Saussure's but committed to a historical approach, described language in Durkheimian terms as 'eminently a social fact ('éminémment un fait social'). He was a semi-determinist who argued that 'Languages serve to express the mentality of the speaking subjects, but each one constitutes a highly organized system which imposes itself on them, which gives their thought its form and only submits to the action of this mentality in a slow and partial manner.'[19]

The French historian Lucien Febvre, a former pupil of Meillet, illustrated his theory of the relation between language and mentality in a study of François Rabelais and the problem of unbelief. In this study, Febvre argued that atheism was impossible in the sixteenth century, among other reasons because of the lack of abstract concepts in French which might sustain such a world-

[15]  Veblen (1899); Hall (1960).
[16]  Bakhtin (1929, 1940). On him, Clark and Holquist (1984), ch. 10.
[17]  Mauthner (1902–3), vol. 3, 4. On him, Kühn (1975), esp. 73ff. On Nietzsche, Strong (1984), ch. 6.
[18]  Whorf (1956).
[19]  Meillet (1921), 16, 210.

view.[20] Earlier in his career, between 1906 and 1924, Febvre had written a number of review articles on the history of language in the *Revue de Synthèse Historique*, praising the work of Meillet and telling historians that they needed to follow what the linguists were doing, for example the study of the introduction of French into the south of France in the centuries before the French Revolution.[21]

The subject was also of great interest to Febvre's friend and colleague Marc Bloch. Indeed, it has been suggested that Bloch learned the comparative method of which he set such store from the linguists, from Meillet in particular.[22] Historians in other countries and other fields – the church historians Gustav Mensching, Jozef Schrijnen and Christine Mohrmann, for example, the Spanish cultural historian Amerigo Castro, and the Swedish historian Nils Ahnlund – were also studying aspects of language and society at about this time.[23]

As for the stage of systematic research, it was reached a generation ago, in the late 1950s and early 1960s, with the development of what has been variously called 'sociolinguistics', 'ethnolinguistics', 'the sociology of language', the 'ethnography of speaking' or 'the ethnography of communication'. In the English-speaking world, the most influential figures include Joshua Fishman, John Gumperz, M. A. K. Halliday, Dell Hymes, and William Labov. The different names for the new discipline or subdiscipline represent substantial differences of approach, macrosociological or microsociological, concerned with 'language' in the wide or the narrow sense. All the same, they should not be allowed to obscure what the different schools have in common, or the relevance of this common body of ideas for social historians.[24]

Since some British, American and German historians have recently taken what has been called a 'linguistic turn' and are now very much concerned with certain aspects of language and communication, it may be worth attempting to define the differ-

---

20    Febvre (1942), 385ff.
21    Brun (1923).
22    Bloch (1939–40), ch. 5, part 2; Walker (1980).
23    Mensching (1926); Schrijnen (1932); Mohrmann (1932); Castro (1941); Ahnlund (1943); Woodbine (1943).
24    Fishman (1972); Gumperz (1972); Gumperz and Hymes (1972); Hymes (1974); Labov (1972a), esp. 183–359. Trudgill (1974) is a lucid introduction to the field.

ence between their approaches and the social history of language recommended (and, I hope, practised) in this volume.

On one side, Hans-Georg Gadamer and Jürgen Habermas are concerned with general theories of hermeneutics and of communicative behaviour. They do not ignore history, but their interest is in the major trends in the history of the modern West, rather than in everyday communication at a local level.[25]

On the other side, in the six massive volumes of their *Grundgeschichtliche Grundbegriffe*, Reinhart Koselleck and his colleagues concern themselves with language as a source for the 'history of concepts' (*Begriffsgeschichte*) rather than with speaking or writing as human activities worthy of historical attention for their own sake.[26] In a similar way to Koselleck, some English-speaking historians of political thought (notably J. G. A. Pocock and Quentin Skinner) have focussed on changes in what they sometimes call the 'language of politics', while social historians have examined the 'language of class' and 'the language of labour'.[27]

My aim here is not to criticize either of these important enterprises, but simply to suggest that there is or ought to be what might be called 'conceptual space' between them for a third approach, more sociological than Koselleck's, Pocock's or Skinner's and more concrete than that of Habermas. This third approach might be summed up as the attempt to add a social dimension to the history of language and a historical dimension to the work of sociolinguists and ethnographers of speaking.

The concern with speech as well as with written communication in the past deserves emphasis. Like the history of popular culture, the historical ethnography of speaking involves a shift of historical interest from the communicative acts of a minority to those of the whole people. As in the case of popular culture, it is difficult to find sources which are both rich and reliable, but sources for the history of speech do exist, as we shall see.

What do these ethnographers and sociologists have to offer historians? They demonstrate an acute awareness of 'who speaks what language to whom and when'.[28] They show that the forms

---

[25]   Gadamer (1965); Habermas (1970). On their debate, Jay (1982).
[26]   Brunner et al. (1972–90); Koselleck (1979). Cf. Grünert (1974).
[27]   Pocock (1972) esp. ch. 1; Pagden (1987); Briggs (1960); Sewell (1980).
[28]   Fishman (1965).

of communication are not neutral bearers of information but carry their own messages. They have put forward a number of theories which historians can test. They have also created a rich analytical vocabulary. Just as the Bedouin have many words for 'camel', and Eskimos for 'snow', because they draw finer distinctions in these areas than most of us need to do, so the sociolinguists have many words for 'language'.

In this vocabulary, a central place is taken by the term 'variety' or 'code'. (The term 'code', used by the structuralists in opposition to 'message', seems to be going out of use because of its ambiguities).[29] A variety may be defined as a way of speaking employed by a particular 'speech community'.[30]

The notion of 'speech community' has been criticized – like other notions of community – for assuming social consensus and ignoring conflict and subordination.[31] To ignore social and linguistic conflict would indeed be mistaken, but the rejection of the idea of community surely goes too far. After all, solidarity and conflict are opposite sides of the same coin. Groups define themselves and forge solidarities in the course of conflict with others (a point which will be argued in more detail on pp. 67–76 below). Hence the validity of this criticism of the idea of 'speech community' depends on the way in which the concept is used. In these pages it will be employed either to describe common features of speech or to refer to individual or group identification with particular speech forms, without making assumptions about the absence of linguistic or other conflict or about the overlap between a community defined in linguistic terms and the social or religious communities to be found in the same region.

Simplifying brutally, as brief introductions inevitably do, it may be suggested that sociolinguists have used this idea of a variety of language to make four main points about the relations between languages and the societies in which they are spoken or written. These points may well seem rather obvious when they are stated in a bare and simple form, but they have not, so far at least, been fully integrated into the practice of social historians. They are as follows:

---

[29]    Halliday (1978), 11
[30]    Gumperz (1972). Cf. Vossler (1924).
[31]    Calvet (1987); Pratt (1987); Williams (1992).

1   Different social groups use different varieties of language.
2   The same individuals employ different varieties of language in different situations.
3   Language reflects the society or culture in which it is used.
4   Language shapes the society in which it is used.

The following pages will comment on these points one by one and offer a few historical illustrations.

(1)   Different social groups use different varieties of language.[32] Regional dialects are perhaps the most obvious example of varieties, which not only reveal differences between communities but also – at least on occasion – express consciousness of these differences, or pride in them. What linguists call 'language loyalty' may also be described as a consciousness of community, at least of what Benedict Anderson has called an 'imagined community'.[33] However, a common speech may coexist with deep social conflicts. A distinctive accent – if nothing else – unites Catholics and Protestants in Northern Ireland, and blacks and whites in South Africa or in the American South.

Some other varieties of language, based on occupation, gender, religion, or other sectors, from football to finance, are known as 'social dialects', 'sociolects', or 'special' or 'sectional' languages (*Sondersprache, langues spéciaux, linguaggi settoriali*).[34] The secret language of professional beggars and thieves (variously known as *Rotwelsch, argot, gergo*, 'cant' and so on) attracted the interest of writers relatively early, and guides to it appeared in print from the sixteenth century onwards.[35] The language of soldiers (say) or lawyers has attracted less attention so far, but deserves extended analysis from this point of view.[36]

Again, the language of women was and is different from that of men in a number of ways. In many societies these differences include a predilection for euphemisms and for emotionally charged adjectives, a rhetoric of hesitancy and indirection, and a closer adherence to standard or 'correct' forms. Women do not simply

---

[32]   On varieties, Saville-Troike (1982), 75ff.
[33]   Labov (1972a); Anderson (1983).
[34]   Devoto (1972); Beccaria (1973).
[35]   Avé-Lallemant (1858–62); Sainéan (1907); Camporesi (1973).
[36]   Fiorelli (1984).

happen to speak differently from men. In many places they have been and are trained to speak differently, to express their social subordination in a hesitant or 'powerless' variety of language.[37] Their intonation as well as their vocabulary and syntax is affected by their perceptions of what men want to hear.[38] As one Shakespearian character remarks of another, 'Her voice was ever soft / Gentle and low, an excellent thing in woman' (*King Lear*, Act 5, Scene 3). Even Mrs Thatcher bowed to this convention when, as prime minister, she took lessons in elocution in order to lower the pitch of her voice.[39]

We are also told that 'Statistical measurements show that men speak more loudly and more often than women; are more apt to interrupt, impose their views, and take over the conversation; and are more inclined to shout others down. Women tend to smile obligingly, excuse themselves and stutter, or in fits of insecurity attempt to imitate and outdo men.'[40] Alternatively, they employ strategies of indirectness, like the wives who practise the art of asking their husbands 'tiny and discreet questions', a point recently made about a village in Spain but one with a much wider relevance, the limits of which future social historians may care to chart.[41]

Again, distinctive varieties of language have often been the mark of religious minorities. In a pioneering study, the Dutch historian Jozef Schrijnen pointed out that the early Christians, like lawyers, soldiers, boatmen and other social groups, employed a *Sondersprache*, a variety of Latin which expressed their solidarity. They coined new terms, such as *baptizare*, or used old terms, such as *carnalis*, in a new sense, and thus 'created a close-knit speech community' ('schuf eine engere Sprachgemeinschaft'), expressing the strong solidarity of a persecuted group.[42]

In late medieval England, the heretics known as Lollards appear to have developed a distinctive vocabulary. In early modern times, the puritans were supposed to be recognizable by their nasal twang as well as by the frequency with which they used terms such as 'pure', 'zeal', or 'carnal', a usage parodied in Ben Jonson's

[37]  Lakoff (1975); Spender (1980); Cameron (1990).
[38]  McConnell-Ginet (1978).
[39]  Atkinson (1984), 113.
[40]  Illich (1983), 135.
[41]  Harding (1975).
[42]  Schrijnen (1932), 5–7. Cf. Mohrmann (1932), 8, and Schrijnen (1939).

play *Bartholomew Fair*.[43] Quakers stood out not only because they insisted on using the familiar 'thee' and 'thou' to everyone, but also by their refusal to use certain common words such as 'church', not to mention their special use of silence in prayer meetings.[44]

Elsewhere in Europe, religious minorities were also recognizable by their speech. According to a sixteenth-century Italian writer, Stefano Guazzo, the French Calvinists or 'Huguenots' could be recognized by their tone of voice, so quiet as to be scarcely audible, as if they were dying. Their speech was so full of biblical phrases that it was known irreverently as 'the dialect of the Promised Land' ('le patois de Canaan').[45] The typical German Pietist, according to the late eighteenth-century critic F. A. Weckherlin, 'whimpers or sighs in a whining, meek and quiet manner' ('weinerlich, sanft und leise wimmert oder seufzt'), as well as employing a distinctive vocabulary with favourite adjectives such as 'liebe' or turns of phrase like 'the fullness of the heart' ('Fülle des Herzens').[46]

Varieties of language are also associated with social class. Given the reputation of the British in such matters, it is no surprise to discover that the best-known discussion concerns the so-called 'U' and 'non-U' forms of English. It was the linguist Alan Ross who coined the term 'U' to describe the language of the British upper class, and 'non-U' for that of everyone else. He explained, or more exactly asserted, that 'looking-glass' was U, while 'mirror' was non-U; 'writing-paper' U, 'note-paper' non-U; 'napkin' U, 'serviette' non-U, and so on.[47] His ideas were taken up and popularized by his friend Nancy Mitford.[48]

Considerable anxiety seems to have been aroused by this discussion, at least in Britain, and a generation later, now that the dispute has passed into history, it might be worth investigating whether linguistic usage changed in some circles as a result. However, such pairs of terms were not new in English usage. In 1907, a writer on etiquette, Lady Grove, was already claiming that one should say 'looking-glass' rather than 'mirror', and

43  Hudson (1981); Beek (1969).
44  Bauman (1983); Lennon (1991).
45  Guazzo (1574), 79.
46  Quoted in Fulbrook (1983), 149; Cf. Langer (1954).
47  Ross (1954).
48  Mitford (1956). Cf. Buckle (1978).

'napkin' rather than 'serviette'.[49] In any case, although they are widely believed to reflect a peculiarly English obsession with class, distinctions of this kind do have parallels in other parts of the world.

In Philadelphia in the 1940s, for instance, it was U to refer to one's 'house' and 'furniture', but non-U to call them 'home' and 'furnishings'; U to feel 'sick', but non-U to feel 'ill'. In similar fashion, Emily Post recommended her readers never to say that someone has an 'elegant home' but to call it a 'beautiful house'.[50] Long before this, in eighteenth-century Denmark, the playwright Ludvig Holberg put a character on stage in his *Erasmus Montanus* (Act 1, Scene 2) to comment on the way in which language was changing to reflect some people's social aspirations or pretentions. 'In my youth people spoke differently here in the hills from the way they do now; where they now speak of a "lackey", they used to say "boy"... a "musician" was called a "player", and a "secretary" a "clerk"' ('I mi Ungdom talede man ikke saa her paa Bierget som nu; det som man nu kalder Lakei, kaldte man da Dreng... en Musikant Spillemand, og en Sikketerer Skriver'). Generations earlier, in seventeenth-century France, François de Callières, later private secretary to Louis XIV, wrote a dialogue called *Mots à la mode* (1693), pointing out differences between what he called 'bourgeois speech styles' ('façons de parler bourgeoises') and patterns characteristic of the aristocracy. One participant, the marquise, declares herself unable to bear a bourgeois lady who calls her husband *mon époux* rather than *mon mari*. Ways of speaking thus reveal 'different social classes' ('espèces de classes différentes').[51]

Earlier still, in sixteenth-century Italy, the writer Pietro Aretino, who rejected the linguistic purism of Pietro Bembo and other humanists because it was unnatural and artificial, mocked it by introducing into one of his dialogues a woman of low status and high pretensions who claimed that a window should be called a *balcone*, and not, as was more common, a *finestra*; that it was proper to say *viso* for 'face' but improper (or non-U) to say *faccia*, and so on. His joke would have had little point if other people had not been taking the matter seriously.[52] In the same

---

[49]  Phillipps (1984), 57–8.
[50]  Baltzell (1958), 51. Cf. Post (1922), 60.
[51]  Callières (1693), 42–3, 65.
[52]  Aretino (1975), 82. Cf. Aquilecchia (1976).

milieu, courtiers seem to have affected a special form of pronunciation, a kind of drawl, criticized by a speaker in Baldassare
Castiglione's famous *Courtier* (book 1, chapter 19) as speaking
'in such a languid manner that they seem at their last gasp' ('così
afflitta, che in quel punto par che lo spirito loro finisca').

It is not only in the West that varieties of speech symbolize
status. In Java, for example, the elite have their own dialect (or
better, 'sociolect'), High Javanese, which is distinctive not only in
its vocabulary but in grammar and syntax as well.[53] Among the
Wolof of West Africa, accent, or more exactly pitch, is a social
indicator. The nobles speak in low-pitched quiet voices, as if they
do not need to make an effort to gain their listener's attention,
while commoners speak in high-pitched loud voices.[54] In a similar
way, an Elizabethan writer on English advised his readers that
'in speaking to a Prince the voice ought to be low and not loud
or shrill, for th'one is a sign of humility, th'other of too much
audacity and presumption.'[55] The parallel with the low voice
which Elizabethan men preferred in their women will be obvious
enough.

From a historian's point of view, it is important to note that
linguistic status symbols are subject to change over time. In
Britain, unlike many other parts of Europe, regional accents have
been non-U for a couple of centuries. However, they were not
always so. At the court of Queen Elizabeth, Sir Walter Ralegh is
said to have spoken with a broad Devonshire accent which did
his career no harm, while Dr Johnson, that arbiter of correct
English, spoke broad Staffordshire.[56]

It does not follow from this propensity to change that the
social symbolism of varieties of language is completely arbitrary.
The American sociologist Thorstein Veblen put forward the
fascinating suggestion that the ways of speaking of an upper class
(or 'leisure class', as he put it) were necessarily 'cumbrous and
out of date' because such usages imply 'waste of time' and
hence 'exemption from the use and need of direct and forcible
speech'.[57] The Wolof example quoted above would seem to
illustrate this point, for which it would not be difficult to amass

[53]    Geertz (1960); Siegel (1986).
[54]    Irvine (1974).
[55]    Puttenham (1589).
[56]    K. V. Thomas's essay on the history of regional accents in Britain remains unpublished.
Cf. Phillipps (1984), 22ff.
[57]    Veblen (1899). Cf. Hall (1960).

many supporting instances. Some sixty years after Veblen, his idea of necessary links between varieties of language and the social groups employing them was reinforced by another socio-logist, Basil Bernstein, whose views have generated considerable controversy.

Studying the language of the pupils in some London schools in the 1950s, Bernstein distinguished two main varieties (or as he called them, 'codes'), the 'elaborated' and the 'restricted'. The restricted code employs concrete expressions and it leaves meanings implicit, to be inferred from the context. In contrast the elaborated code is abstract, explicit and 'context-independent'. Bernstein explained the contrast in terms of two different styles of childrearing, associated with two types of family and two social classes. Broadly speaking, the elaborated code is middle class while the restricted code is working class.[58]

Originally designed to explain the relative failure of working-class children to achieve good grades at school, Bernstein's theory has much wider implications, especially for the relationship between language and thought explored by Whorf and others. From the point of view of a historian of mentalities, there are intriguing similarities between the two codes and the contrasts which have so often been drawn between two styles of thought, whether they are labelled 'primitive' and 'civilised', 'traditional' and 'modern', 'prelogical' and 'logical', or (rather more usefully, in my view) 'oral' and 'literate'.[59]

Bernstein's remarks about British children aroused a storm of criticism, claiming, for example, that he had suggested that individuals are prisoners of the code they use and that he had emphasized the weaknesses of the working-class code while stressing the positive features of the middle-class one.[60] Some of these criticisms certainly hit the target. All the same, Bernstein's hypotheses about the manners in which styles of speech and styles of thought are acquired in childhood remain extremely stimulating and suggestive.

The fundamental question for historians remains that of explaining how and why some languages or varieties of language have spread (geographically or socially), or have been success-

---

[58]  Bernstein (1971). Cf. Halliday (1978), ch. 5.
[59]  Goody (1977).
[60]  Rosen (1972); Labov (1972b), 213.

fully imposed in the course of time, while others have receded. Linguists have become increasingly interested in this problem in recent years, and it would seem to be a promising area for interdisciplinary cooperation.[61]

(2) One conclusion from these recent studies of language spread is the need to study people who speak more than one language or variety of language and to discover the uses to them of these different forms of speech. This brings us to the second of our four points: that in different situations, the same individual will employ different varieties of language, different 'speech genres', as Bakhtin called them, or as the sociolinguists now say, different 'registers'.[62] It may well be the case, for instance, that the elaborated and restricted 'codes' which Bernstein discovered should be described as 'registers' in this sense, in other words the servants rather than the masters of the individuals employing them.[63]

It was along these lines that Bakhtin criticized Saussure for ignoring the creativity and adaptability of ordinary speech. This adaptability undermines the idea of language as a 'prison' constraining the behaviour of its users, just as it subverts the idea of strict 'rules' with which we are programmed by our culture. Instead it lends support to Pierre Bourdieu's more flexible idea of 'habitus', defined as the 'principle of regulated improvisations', and to Erving Goffman's argument that situations influence the behaviour of individuals as much as the social groups to which they belong.[64]

An example which might repay study from this point of view is the language of tombstones. A historian concerned with nineteenth-century nationalism might be tempted to read Swedish tombstones in Finland (say) or German tombstones in Bohemia as evidence of local language loyalty, but he or she would be well advised to consider the possibility that speakers of Finnish or Czech might have considered Swedish and German the appropriate languages in that particular context, as Latin had been in earlier centuries.

[61] Brosnahan (1963); J. Fishman, 'Language Maintenance and Language Shift', in Fishman (1972); Cooper (1982); Wardhaugh (1987).
[62] On 'speech genres', Bakhtin (1952–3); on 'registers', Hymes (1974) and Halliday (1978), 31ff.
[63] Lakoff (1990), 99–100.
[64] Bourdieu (1972), 78; Goffman (1961). Cf. Hymes (1974).

Some nineteenth-century novelists, Thomas Hardy for example, were aware of the existence of different registers. The heroine of Hardy's *Tess of the Durbervilles* (1891) is described as speaking 'two languages', in other words the Dorset dialect at home and standard English to people of higher status.

Sociolinguists have developed this point by analysing what they call the 'strategies', conscious or unconscious, employed in shifting or 'switching' from one register to another.[65] Their studies of bilingual individuals and communities have shown that people change from one language to another not in an arbitrary or random manner but according to the participants in the conversation and even the topic under discussion, the 'speech domain' as sociolinguists call it.[66] The same observation is true of what is known as 'diglossia', in other words switches between registers. Religion, for example, often seems to demand a relatively 'high' or formal register, such as classical Arabic in the case of Islam.[67]

Historians should have no difficulty in finding examples from many periods of the use of different languages or registers in different speech domains. In the world of late antiquity, for instance, Greek was the language of science and art, even for people who habitually spoke Latin.[68] In the Middle Ages, French was the language of chivalry, and was sometimes used in this domain by people who normally spoke English or Venetian (below, p. 77). French was also the language of the English law in the later Middle Ages, leaving traces on legal usage which are still noticeable.[69] The polyglot emperor Charles V is said to have remarked that French was the language to use to ambassadors (or to flatter), Italian to ladies (or to friends), German to stable-boys (or to threaten), and Spanish to speak to God. (The anecdote has many variants. The earliest known version, from 1601, goes as follows: 'Si loqui cum Deo oporteret, se Hispanice locuturum . . . si cum amicis, Italice . . . si cui blandiendum esset, Gallice . . . si cui minandum . . . Germanice.')[70] French was becoming the language of European diplomacy by the late seventeenth

---

[65]  Gumperz (1982a).
[66]  Fishman (1972).
[67]  Ferguson (1959).
[68]  Mohrmann (1958–61), 103–11.
[69]  Woodbine (1943).
[70]  Quoted in Weinrich (1985), 190.

century, when it was observed that the envoys to the congress of Nijmegen spoke that language 'almost as often as their mother tongues' (but cf. pp. 52–3 below).

Latin was for centuries a second language employed by clerical and lay elites for a variety of reasons in several different speech domains (as the following chapter will show). French too was a second language in a number of European regions. In England and in southern Italy in the fourteenth century (as a result of the Norman conquests), in the Dutch Republic in the seventeenth and eighteenth centuries, in Prussia in the eighteenth century, and in Russia – as *War and Peace* reminds us – in the nineteenth century, speaking French was U.[71] In similar fashion German was U in Bohemia in the seventeenth and eighteenth centuries because it was the language of the court, which was settling down in Vienna. It was also U in Denmark, while Danish in turn was U in Norway (which was ruled from Copenhagen till 1814).

Of course elites were not the only groups to speak more than one language. In seventeenth-century Amsterdam, the Portuguese Jewish community spoke Portuguese or Spanish among themselves, Dutch to outsiders, and Hebrew in the synagogue.[72] On linguistic frontiers bilingualism was and is common. People living near major trade routes have often learned a pidgin or lingua franca, such as Malay in the East Indian archipelago, Swahili in East Africa, Tupi, the so-called *lingua geral*, in Brazil, or the language of trade in the Mediterranean world from which the general term 'lingua franca' is derived, a romance language relatively well documented for North Africa in the nineteenth century but one which has left fragments of written evidence as early as the fourteenth century.[73] The Latin spoken by innkeepers and coachmen in East-Central Europe (below, p. 54–5) may have been a pidgin of this kind. In the ancient Mediterranean world, this function was performed by Greek, the so-called *koiné*. Elsewhere, communication sometimes took place in a mixture of languages, like the germanized Italian or italianized German spoken by the German troops in Italy in the sixteenth century.[74] These

[71] W. Frijhoff of the University of Rotterdam is working on a study of French in the Netherlands.
[72] Swetschinski (1982), 56–7.
[73] Drewes (1929); Whinnom (1977). Cf. Folena (1968–70).
[74] Coates (1969).

striking examples of heteroglossia suggest that historians should study not only 'the linguistics of community' but also what has been called the 'linguistics of contact', in other words 'the workings of language across rather than within lines of social differentiation'.[75]

The religious domain in Christendom as well as Islam has often been marked by the use of a special language, in Protestant areas as well as Catholic ones. In seventeenth-century Languedoc, where Occitan was still spoken by most people for everyday purposes, the Huguenots preferred French as the language of their liturgy. When the French Protestants were persecuted in the late seventeenth century and a movement of resistance was organized in the Cevennes, some of its leaders, more especially the women, would not infrequently fall into convulsions and prophesy. When they did so, they employed French, not their everyday Occitan.[76] For them, French was a linguistic symbol of the sacred, effective in this respect – like Latin for most Catholics – whether the congregation understood it or not. There is an obvious parallel with glossolalia, from New Testament times to our own.[77]

Switching between dialect and a literary language is also well documented in some regions and periods. In early modern Italy, for example, educated men were able to speak as well as to write Tuscan, but they continued to employ their local dialect on occasion, although there has been little attempt so far to study these occasions or domains in a systematic way. In the state of Venice, for example, Venetian was still employed as the language of the courts in the eighteenth century, perhaps because it symbolised the republic's independence.[78]

Conversely, in nineteenth-century France, peasants who normally spoke patois might switch register into French on special occasions. One of the few historians to have taken this subject seriously so far, Eugen Weber, tells us that a boy might employ French as a sign of formality when inviting a girl to dance, and also that peasants who discussed local politics in patois would switch to French to talk about national issues.[79]

---

[75]    Pratt (1987).
[76]    Le Roy Ladurie (1966), 279.
[77]    Samarin (1972).
[78]    Vianello (1957).
[79]    Weber (1976), ch. 6.

Unfortunately, our knowledge of such matters remains fragmentary. It is interesting to learn that Venetian patricians (notably Maffeo Venier) wrote erotic poetry in dialect, or that Lord Tennyson used to tell bawdy stories in a Lincolnshire accent (a regional accent which, unlike Ralegh and Johnson, he did not employ the rest of the time), but these pieces of information are not fully intelligible without a knowledge of their contexts, including a knowledge of the rules for speaking in those cultures. Ethnographers of speaking have been investigating these rules – how to be polite or insulting, how to joke, how to ask for a drink and so on – but their example has not been followed by many social historians.[80] Even silence deserves study from this point of view, as the final chapter will try to demonstrate.

Without this kind of knowledge of linguistic rules, explicit or implicit, historians run a serious risk of misinterpreting many of their documents, which are not as transparent or unproblematic as they are frequently assumed to be. Form communicates. As the Canadian critic Marshall McLuhan used to say, 'the medium is the message.'[81] More exactly, the medium, code, variety or register employed is a crucial part of the message, which a historian cannot afford to neglect.

Obvious examples are the forms of politeness or impoliteness current in a particular milieu at a particular time. It may well be the case that the fundamental strategies of politeness remain constant across cultures and therefore, presumably, over time as well.[82] However, at a level which is more superficial – but not to be neglected – trends over time seem relatively easy to discern. In the case of Italy in the sixteenth and seventeenth centuries, for example, the records suggest a trend towards what might be called the 'inflation' of polite forms, or the debasement of the verbal currency. Honorific terms of address such as *Messer* or *Signora* came to be used to a widening circle of people, leading those of higher status to invent or appropriate still more impressive titles.

In the early seventeenth century, for instance, the Genoese patrician Andrea Spinola, a staunch defender of republican

---

[80]   Two classic ethnographic studies are Labov (1972b) and Frake (1972). I have tried to follow my own advice in Burke (1987), notably in chs 7–9.
[81]   McLuhan (1964), ch. 1.
[82]   Brown and Levinson (1987).

values, complained about deferential greetings such as 'your slave' (*vostro schiavo*, compare the Hungarian *Szervusz*) or 'I kiss your hands' (*bacio le mani*, compare the Hungarian *kezét csokolom* and the Spanish *beso sus manos*).[83] At much the same time, the political writer Traiano Boccalini, a strong opponent of Spanish rule in Italy, blamed the Spaniards for the spread of titles. 'The title of *Magnificent* or *Magnanimous*, which is only suitable for princes and heroes, is now barely acceptable by merchants. *Illustrious*, which is not inappropriate for emperors, generals and men of distinction, is used of ordinary citizens as well.'[84] Later in the century a Florentine patrician, Tommaso Rinuccini, complained of the new fashion for calling everyone 'most illustrious' (*illustrissimo*) so that 'even ordinary people use it to gentlemen, even the poor when they beg for alms'.[85] Some observers interpreted the change as an example of the influence of Spain on Italian (below, p. 87).

As in the case of politeness, there was a rich vocabulary of insult in early modern Italy, though it seems to have been slower to change over time (could this be because insults are the domain of the id, politeness that of the superego?). In this society as in many others, insults, a breach of the rules in one sense of the term, in another sense followed rules or conventions almost as closely as a sonnet. They were stereotyped, or as William Labov puts it, 'ritualized'.[86] As in the case of the sonnet, however, these rules allowed considerable scope for creativity and invention, as I have tried to show elsewhere in a study of written insults in seventeenth-century Rome, which offered many ingenious variations on the theme of 'cuckold' (*becco*).[87]

The written language is another obvious example of a register, for it is generally more like a translation than a transcription of the spoken language. Writing is a separate variety of language with its own rules, varying with time, place, writer, intended reader, topic (domain) and, not least, literary genre – including in this literary category of 'genre' such everyday forms as letters of various types – the love letter, the begging letter, the threatening letter, and so on.[88]

---

[83]  Burke (1987), 88.
[84]  Boccalini (1678), vol. 1, 38.
[85]  Rinuccini (1863).
[86]  Labov (1972b), 297–353. Cf. Dundes, Leach and Özkök (1972); Flynn (1977).
[87]  Burke (1987), 95–109.
[88]  Basso (1974). On the threatening letter, Thompson (1975).

In eleventh-century Japan, for example, the 'next morning letter' from a courtly lover to the mistress from whom he had just parted was not only *de rigueur*, but had to be composed according to strict rules which governed not only the poem which formed the heart of the message but also the calligraphy, the choice of paper, and even the spray of blossom to which the letter, properly folded, was attached.[89] In traditional China, the distinctive forms of official documents, from calligraphy to formulae, were taken as the models for messages addressed to the world of spirits, which was imagined to be organized into a 'heavenly bureaucracy', communicating only through the proper channels.[90]

One of the most immediate tasks for social historians of language is to discover who, in a given place and time, used the medium of writing to communicate with whom about what. Sixteenth-century Venetians, for example, seem to have preferred not to comment on political matters in writing, for reasons of prudence. The sixteenth-century merchant Gianbattista Donà once reprimanded his son for writing to him (during his absence from Venice on business) about politics, or as he put it, *cose di signori*.[91] Much of popular culture failed to be recorded in writing, not only because many ordinary people could not write, but also because the literate were either uninterested in popular culture, or ashamed of that interest, or simply unable to transcribe an oral culture into the written form of the language. When it was eventually written down, certain features of this oral culture were omitted, not only to accommodate it to middle-class readers, but also to the medium of writing.[92]

Since there are so many lacunae, readers may well wonder whether a social history of speaking is a viable enterprise, at least before the coming of the tape-recorder. However, in the case of western Europe from the later Middle Ages onwards, there are some extremely voluminous and relatively reliable sources for speech, notably the records of the courts, where care was often taken to ask witnesses to testify to the exact words spoken on particular occasions. The Inquisition went especially far in this direction. The instructions given to the Roman inquisitors of the

---

[89]  Morris (1964), 187ff.
[90]  Ahern (1981), ch. 2.
[91]  Venice, Biblioteca Correr, ms Donà 418, i, 5.
[92]  Details in Burke (1978), ch. 3.

seventeenth century, for example, told them to ensure that the notary, who had to be present at all interrogations, transcribed 'not only all the responses of the accused but also all the other remarks and comments he made and every word he uttered under torture, including every sigh, scream, groan and sob' ('E procureranno i Giudici, che il notaro scriva non solamente tutte le risposte del Reo ma anco tutti i ragionamenti e moti, che farò e tutte le parole ch'egli proferirà ne'tormenti, anzi tutti i sospiri, tutte le grida, tutti i lamenti, e le lagrime che mandera').[93] A chilling directive, but one which has been invaluable for historians.

In other contexts too, the representation of speech in writing seems to have been remarkably accurate. It was not uncommon for the sermons of distinguished preachers, such as San Bernardino of Sienna or Jean Calvin, to be transcribed by members of the audience, sometimes in shorthand. Records were made of speeches in assemblies such as the English House of Commons long before the professionalism of Hansard, who began to print the journals of the House of Commons in 1774.[94] There were also attempts to write down the conversation of distinguished individuals, such as Martin Luther or John Selden, usually during meals, so that the genre was known as 'table-talk'. Given the circumstances, it is unlikely that these records are completely accurate, but they certainly have a colloquial flavour.

To these sources may be added the evidence of plays and novels. They have to be used with care because novelists and dramatists generally stylize speech rather than reproducing it exactly, but to anyone aware of these conventions they can be extremely informative. As the editor of *The Oxford Book of English Talk* remarked, some forty years ago, 'If we wish to know how Englishmen spoke in the days of Queen Elizabeth or Queen Victoria, we must rely for the most part on the imaginative writers, the dramatists and the novelists.' (In fact he also made good use of the reports of trials.)[95]

In short, studies of the uses and conventions of literacy, still much too rare, are a necessary complement to the numerous quantitative studies of literacy carried out in the last few years.

---

[93] Masini (1665), p. 157. For a famous example, see Firpo (1985), 196ff., 214ff.
[94] Notestein (1935).
[95] Sutherland (1953), v.

They raise problems which all historians need to take seriously, for without awareness of these constantly changing conventions, it is impossible to tell whether a given text is serious or ironic, servile or mocking, whether it follows the rules or subverts them.

The first two sociolinguistic themes are essentially descriptive. The remaining two are more analytical and also more controversial.

(3)  Language reflects (or better, 'echoes') society.[96] In the first place, the accent, vocabulary and general speech style of an individual reveals, to anyone with a trained ear, a good deal about that individual's place in society. In the second place, linguistic forms, their variations and changes tell us something about the nature of the totality of social relationships in a given culture. In his history of the English family, Lawrence Stone argued for a change in attitudes to marriage among the upper classes at the end of the seventeenth century, using as one of his sources of evidence the abandonment of formal modes of address (such as 'Sir' and 'Madam') between husbands and wives, 'and the adoption of first names and terms of endearment'.[97] In a similar way, but with considerably more detail and depth, a recent study of the Italian family uses changes in language – in the use of *tu*, *voi* and *lei* for example – in order to write the history of deference, detachment, familiarity and so on.[98]

A particularly useful 'litmus paper', revealing patterns of familiarity and deference, power and solidarity, is the use of *tu* and *vous* in French, *Du* and *Sie* in German, *Ty* and *Vy* in Russian, and equivalent terms in other languages. The two terms (T and V, as they are generally called for convenience in cross-language comparisons) may be used either reciprocally or non-reciprocally, with very different meanings in the two cases. Usage has tended to vary with the relative status and intimacy of the speakers (and also, in Russian, at least, with the topic of conversation). As might have been expected, the rules for the use of T and V in different European languages have changed over time, especially in the course of the last generation, with a general shift

[96]  An unusually explicit use of this metaphor of reflection is Vossler (1913).
[97]  Stone (1977), 329ff.
[98]  Barbagli (1984), 273ff.

to reciprocity which indicates the spread of more egalitarian values.[99]

However, the detailed history of the changes in each language (and indeed each region and each social group) remains to be studied. It is interesting to discover Aretino's Nanna telling her pupil Pippa to use *voi* because 'that *tu* has a dry sound' ('quel "tu" ha del secco') or to learn that in the Piarist schools of the seventeenth century, pupils were expected to address one another in the same way, while in the Jesuit college of Bologna, the teachers 'do not use *tu* to anyone, for whatever reason, but call everyone *voi*' ('a niuno per qualsiasi cosa danno del tu, indifferentemente a tutti del voi'). To assess the significance of such details, however, much more research is needed.[100]

It is for future social historians to chart the exact chronology, geography and sociology of this shift, as well as to interpret the specific overtones or undertones of usage in particular contexts, distinguishing (if possible) the genuinely deferential from the patronizing or ironic usages. All the same, we have learned something about social relationships in fourteenth-century Languedoc now that we have been told that a parish priest would use T to his flock, but receive V in return.[101] We have been helped to assess the significance of some rural revolts in nineteenth-century India by writers who describe with horror, or at least with surprise, the use of T by peasants to their lords and masters, instead of the customary V.[102] We have discovered something significant about social change and attitudes to change in nineteenth-century Russia when we read, in Turgenev's *Smoke*, that Litvinov's mother (a member of the provincial nobility) addressed her servants with V, instead of the traditional T, because she believed that this was the progressive, western thing to do, just as we have a sudden insight into relationships between the sexes among the nineteenth-century Russian aristocracy when we learn that Tolstoy's wife Sonia was afraid to say T to her husband on her wedding night.[103]

That these pronouns were heavily charged with social meaning

---

[99]    The classic sociolinguistic study is Brown and Gilman (1960).
[100]    Aretino (1975); Liebreich (1985); Adami (1946), 27.
[101]    Le Roy Ladurie (1975), 515.
[102]    Guha (1983), 49ff.
[103]    Cf. Friedrich (1966); Lyons (1980).

became particularly clear whenever the system, social and linguistic, was challenged, as it was by the Quakers, for example, when they used T to address everyone regardless of their worldly status. A similar point was made by the use of T and of *citoyen* and *citoyenne* during the French Revolution, and by the Saminists in Java at the end of the nineteenth century, a group who rejected both the social hierarchy and the traditionally strict linguistic etiquette of the region and replaced conventional modes of address by the term *sedular* or 'brother'.[104] The parallel with attempts by contemporary feminists to reform our male-dominated language ('mankind', 'chairman', etc.) will be obvious enough, and it is another reminder of the symbolic importance of the apparently trivial.

Modes of address are not the only linguistic clues to social relationships. The choice of a particular variety of language conveys information about the speaker's loyalties, expressing solidarity with those who speak in the same way and distance from those who speak differently. The well-known phenomenon of 'colonial lag', in other words the persistence of traditional forms of language in the colonies long after they have been abandoned in the metropolis, should perhaps be interpreted in terms of collective nostalgia rather than reduced to a mere effect of slow communications. Again, when the upper classes of western Europe gave up using the local dialect – as they generally did in the course of the seventeenth and eighteenth centuries – they were distancing themselves from a popular culture in which their ancestors had participated.[105]

In similar fashion, the development of certain social dialects, for example the occupational languages of the law, the army and the civil service, or of religious groups like Puritans and Pietists, needs to be explained not only in a utilitarian way, as the creation of technical terms for precise practical purposes, but also in a symbolic way, as the expression of a growing group self-consciousness and of a growing sense of distance from the rest of society. The slang of professional beggars and thieves is an extreme case of this creation of a symbolic boundary between a single group and the rest of society. It has been interpreted as an

104  Bauman (1983); Scott (1976), 237.
105  Burke (1978), ch. 9.

'antilanguage' which 'brings into sharp relief the role of language as a realisation of the power structure of society', and at the same time reflects the organization and values of a 'counterculture'.[106]

Whether 'reflection' is an altogether appropriate metaphor for the relations between languages and societies is, however, open to question. A more appropriate visual image might be 'refraction', with its implication that the relation is indirect.

One point which might be made against the reflection theory is that linguistic conventions often persist after changes in the social structures they are supposed to reflect. In Poland, for example, forms of politeness once confined to the nobility have passed into general currency, and it is customary to address strangers as *Pan* and *Pani* ('Sir' and 'Madam') whatever their apparent social status. After the Second World War the Communist Party attempted to sweep this custom away, along with much else, and to replace it by *Wy* (modelled on the Russian form of V). However, this innovation was not generally accepted – for reasons which it would be politically naive to reduce to the power of 'tradition'. The consequence, unintended by all groups, was that the use of *Wy* became a badge of party membership.[107]

(4)   In any case, both 'reflection' and 'refraction' carry the misleading implication that the role of language in society is a purely passive one. My last thesis (echoing sociolinguistics once more) is that speaking is a form of doing, that language is an active force in society, a means for individuals and groups to control others or to resist such control, for changing society or for blocking change, for affirming or suppressing cultural identities (a point discussed at greater length in chapter 3).[108]

This thesis about the power of language may be seen as a positive transvaluation of Nietzsche's critique of epistemology.[109] It does not refer merely to one specialized form of language which has been taken relatively seriously by historians – the language of official propaganda. The point is that the social history of language, like other forms of social history, cannot be divorced from questions of power.[110]

[106]   Halliday (1978), ch. 9.
[107]   Davies (1984), 9.
[108]   Brenneis and Myers (1984), 1–2; Le Page and Tabouret-Keller (1985).
[109]   Strong (1984).
[110]   Bloch (1975), introduction; Payne (1981).

In eighteenth-century England, for example, reading the Riot Act to a group whom the authorities considered to be rioters was 'an exercise of power' in the sense that (according to the provisions of this law) the action of reading made the group liable to execution if they did not disperse within an hour.[111] In similar fashion, the reading of the so-called *Requerimiento*, a document – in Spanish – requiring the hearers to submit to the authority of the king of Spain, authorized the use of force against the indigenous inhabitants of the Americas if they did not obey.[112] Again, as the late Michel Foucault and American 'labelling theorists' have emphasized, the act of describing individuals as 'insane', 'witches', 'criminals' and so on changes the behaviour of other individuals towards them and may even call new groups into existence.[113]

A dramatic illustration of the active force of language is the insult, a form of aggression in which adjectives or nouns are used not so much to describe another person as to strike that person. In seventeenth-century Rome, as elsewhere in the Mediterranean world, it was common to insult men by calling them cuckolds, and women by calling them whores. Such characterizations are unlikely to have had much to do with the social behaviour of the victims. They were simply the best means to annihilate the reputation of the victims, to bring about their social destruction.[114]

At a more general level, it is frequently argued by linguists, sociologists and historians alike that language plays a central part in the 'social construction of reality', that it creates or 'constitutes' society as well as being created by society. To expose the power of language is one of the principal aims of the current movement of 'deconstruction'. Jacques Derrida, for example, suggests that language uses its speakers rather than the other way round. We are the servants rather than the masters of our metaphors (including this one).[115] His suggestion has its parallels in Foucault's emphasis on discourse at the expense of individual speakers and in Claude Lévi-Strauss's aphorism that we do not think with myths, but myths think themselves in us, as well as in the ideas of Whorf, Mauthner and Nietzsche, discussed above.

[111]  Goodrich (1986), v.
[112]  Greenblatt (1991), 97–8.
[113]  Foucault (1961); Cicourel (1973).
[114]  Moogk (1979); Burke (1987), 95–109; Garrioch (1987).
[115]  Derrida (1972).

These arguments certainly have their force, and they expose
the weaknesses of any simplistically instrumental view of language
as a mere tool in the hands, or rather mouths, of its users.
However, like most attempts to turn common sense upside-down,
the counter-arguments have their own weaknesses. They too are
simplistic, and fail to make important distinctions. Some people
seem to have more control of language than others, and a greater
ability to control others by means of language. One thinks of the
many groups of professional communicators in contemporary
society – copywriters, speech-writers, scriptwriters, journalists
and so on, whose job is to sell anything from soap powder to
presidents to their viewers, listeners and readers. Their style is
unmistakably that of the late twentieth century, the age of the
'commercial'. All the same, cultural historians should have no
difficulty in placing these groups in a tradition which includes
such specialists in the art of persuasion as Greek sophists,
Renaissance humanists, and eighteenth-century quack doctors.[116]

It would be unwise to assume either that these professional
persuaders believed all their own propaganda or that they were
all cynically detached from it. We need a term to apply to some
of the situations in between these two extremes, situations in
which individuals are in a sense both masters and servants of
their language. One such term is 'ideology', especially if we
follow the late Louis Althusser and define the term in the relatively
wide sense of the imagined relationship of individuals to their
real conditions of existence.[117]

Another is 'cultural hegemony', used by Antonio Gramsci in
his famous contrast between the two possible ways in which
the ruling class dominates the subordinate classes, with or without the use of force.[118] The trouble with the phrase 'cultural
hegemony' is that it has widened its meaning since Gramsci's day
and is currently employed to refer to almost every society,
whether or not the rulers employ coercion, whether or not they
are involved in persuading the subordinate classes of the legit-
imacy of their rule.

However they choose to describe the problem, it is clear that
social historians need to think seriously about the active role of

---

[116]   On humanists, Seigel (1966); on quacks, Porter (1987).
[117]   Althusser (1970).
[118]   Bennett (1981) 191–218.

language in the creation of the changing social reality they study. Some of the examples discussed in earlier sections of this chapter lend themselves to reinterpretation in these active terms. Feminist linguists have pointed out that ordinary language, male dominated as it is, not only expresses the subordinate place of women but keeps them in a subordinate position.[119] Again, the master using the familiar T to a servant who replies with the deferential V is not merely expressing or symbolizing the social hierarchy but re-enacting, confirming or reproducing it. So is the servant, unless he or she manages to inject a measure of irony into the respectful verbal forms.

Similarly, the technical languages of particular professions and crafts should be interpreted, at least on occasion, not only as reflections of their members' sense of distance from other people, but also as a means of excluding other people, of ensuring that outsiders stay outside. The inhabitants of Polish prisons, according to a recent study, show their awareness of the power of language by compelling new inmates to learn the prison jargon (known as *grypserka*), just as new pupils in British public schools (notably Winchester) were and are compelled by the older boys to learn and use the school slang. The compulsion makes evident the function of a private language in the socialization of the new recruits to the community.[120]

In a similar manner, on a much grander scale, governments have become aware of the uses of standard languages, as opposed to dialects, in the process of state building. From 1789 onwards, as recent studies make abundantly clear, the French government in particular has been particularly conscious of the politics of language and concerned to ensure that all the inhabitants of the hexagon spoke or at any rate understood French.[121] Similarly, the attempts at the erosion of Gaelic, Occitan, Catalan and other 'dominated languages' were an essential part of the process by which the regions where these languages were spoken were sub-jected to the rule of London, Paris, Madrid and so on.[122] In the early eighteenth century, for example, Catalan was under attack

[119] Lakoff (1975).
[120] Halliday (1978), 164.
[121] De Certeau et al. (1975); Lartichaux (1977); Higonnet (1980); Lyons (1981); Boyer and Gardy (1985); Flaherty (1987).
[122] There is a large literature on this subject, including Wall (1969); Gardy (1978); Jones (1980); Durkacz (1983); Grillo (1989a).

in France (where it was spoken in the newly acquired provinces of Cerdagne and Roussillon) as well as in Spain. In Spanish Catalonia, Castilian was made the language of the courts in 1716, and of the schools in 1768. As a leading Catalan intellectual, Antoni de Capmany, wrote at the time – in Castilian – the Catalan language was now 'dead for the republic of letters' and restricted to the sphere of private life.[123]

Sociolinguistics has sometimes been criticized for neglecting domination.[124] There is, however, a growing literature, to which historians and linguists have both made contributions, concerned with the 'colonization of language', for instance the spread of Spanish to the Americas, of English to India, Africa, Australia, etc., of Portuguese to Brazil, Goa, Angola, and so on.[125] Dutch seems to be the exception to this rule, despite a proclamation in Ceylon in 1659 to the effect that no man was allowed to wear a hat unless he could speak Dutch.[126] For example, the Dutch do not seem to have been interested in introducing their language to Indonesia. Indeed, some administrators actively discouraged their subordinates from speaking it.[127] Afrikaans in Africa was the language of settlement rather than empire.

Conversely, the revivals of dominated languages, like Gaelic, may be studied as a part of movements of resistance to central governments perceived by many of their subjects as alien powers.[128] There is equal need for a study of the alternative strategy, the appropriation of dominant languages to resist dominant nations and classes. In East Africa, for instance, Swahili, a traditional lingua franca encouraged by the British (like the Belgians in the Congo) because it facilitated local administration, was given a new function during the independence movement since it turned out to be a useful means of uniting people from different tribes in a common political enterprise, and of encouraging a common consciousness.[129] Ironically enough, English – another

---

[123]  Balcells (1980), 39–46.
[124]  Fabian (1986), 142. Cf. Smith (1984); Andersen (1988); Crowley (1989); Fairclough (1989); Grillo (1989b); Williams (1992).
[125]  General discussions in Brosnahan (1963); Calvet (1974); Fabian (1986); and Kiernan (1991). On Spanish, Wagner (1920, 1949); Castro (1941); Heath (1972); Rosenblatt (1977); Heath and Laprade (1982). On English, Ramson (1970); Mazrui (1978); Cohn (1985). On Portuguese, Rodrigues (1985).
[126]  Drewes (1929), 140.
[127]  Lombard (1990), 79, 134.
[128]  MacDonagh (1983), ch. 7.
[129]  Whiteley (1969); Cf. Fabian (1986).

lingua franca – played a similar role in the break-up of the British Empire. The language of the rulers became the language of resistance in India and in parts of Africa, because it allowed people from different regions to communicate.

Finally, the active role of language can be illustrated from recent studies of the 'rhetoric' or 'discourse' of protest and revolution, studies which take words much more seriously than historians of political movements used to do. Thus Gareth Stedman Jones has criticized earlier social interpretations of the English Chartist movement as 'reductionist' because they neglected the language of the participants. 'Consciousness', he argues against Edward Thompson and others, 'cannot be related to experience except through the interposition of a particular language which organizes the understanding of experience.'[130] Historians of the French Revolution have also expressed dissatisfaction with a reductionist view of language, as a mask for class interests for example, and have suggested that its place in the revolution should be understood as a means of national integration, or as a substitute for power, or as part of a new political culture in which words like *patrie* has a 'magical quality'.[131]

The new sociocultural history has often been criticized on the grounds that it neglects politics and power. The last few examples suggest that there is no need for this neglect, and that the history of language is an area where political, social and cultural historians can and should join forces. It may be useful to end this introductory essay with some suggestions for future research in this politico-linguistic domain, in two areas in particular.

The first is the history of language planning, language reform, language policy or language management, especially on the part of the state. Government concern with language is characteristic of the modern state. Official languages are established in new states (Swahili in Tanzania, for example). The demands by speakers of minority languages to have their children taught in that language or to have newspapers or television channels in it have become major political issues in many parts of the world, from Spain to Romania and from Belgium to Canada.

The obvious historical question to ask at this point is, how long have states regarded the languages spoken by their citizens

[130]   Stedman Jones (1983), 101.
[131]   Furet (1978); Hunt (1984), ch. 1.

as part of their business? The equally obvious answer would seem to be, since the rise of nationalism at the end of the eighteenth century and the association between language and national identity formulated by Herder and other intellectuals at that time. The linguistic politics of the French Revolution offer a spectacular and well-studied example of the involvement of the state in this domain.[132] However, it would seem that language policies had already been formulated by the counter-reformation church, before becoming a matter of secular concern in the age of nationalism.[133] In the nineteenth century, language issues formed part of political debates not only in Europe but also in Japan after the imperial restoration.[134] In the twentieth century, they have spread still more widely. A famous example is Turkey's adoption of the western alphabet in 1928, not only a symbol of westernization but a powerful means of cutting the Turks off from their Ottoman past.[135] Yet these debates have received relatively little attention so far from historians as opposed to linguists. It would be good to see a comparative study, or series of studies, identifying the governments which first took an interest in the languages of their subjects, the individuals and groups in these governments (or indeed outside them) who concerned themselves with language planning, language reform or the management of language conflict, and the effectiveness of the policies actually implemented.

A second area which seems ripe for research is that of the language or languages of government. As we have seen, multi-lingual empires have often tried to conduct their administration in one dominant language – Latin in the Roman Empire, Persian in the Mughal Empire, Quechua in the Inca Empire, and so on. More difficult to study is the process by which particular varieties of administrative language have developed in certain states, from ancient Rome onwards.[136] A well-known example is the 'service language' (*Dienstsprache*) or the 'fiscal German' (*ärarisch Deutsch*) of the eighteenth-century Habsburg Empire.[137] These adminis-

---

[132] De Certeau et al. (1975); Lartichaux (1977); Higonnet (1980); Lyons (1981); Flaherty (1987).
[133] Heath (1972).
[134] Hunter (1988); Cf, Miller (1971).
[135] Karpat (1984).
[136] Macmullen (1962).
[137] Craig (1982).

trative dialects sometimes adopted foreign terms. In the age of Spanish dominance, for example, the *linguaggio cancelleresco* of Milan – the *gergo segretariesco*, as the Italian novelist Alessandro Manzoni later called it – included hybrid Spanish-Italian words such as *papeli* for 'papers' or *veedore* for 'inspector'.[138] Neologisms were also frequent, especially in the nineteenth century: *centralizzare*, for example, *funzionario, insubordinazione*.

Such terms need to be analysed not only from a utilitarian point of view but also from a symbolic one. They helped to create an administrative view of the world and to unite civil servants, but at the price of separating them from the rest of the population, who did not understand the new language or who (like the Italian poet Vincenzo Monti) regarded it as a 'barbarous dialect unfortunately introduced into public administration' ('barbaro dialetto miseramente introdotto nelle pubbliche amministrazioni').[139] They offer one more example of the active role of language in society, and remind us that that role is not necessarily a beneficial one.

---

[138]  Beccaria (1968), 39ff.
[139]  Quoted in Durante (1981), 224.

# 2

## 'Heu Domine, Adsunt Turcae': a Sketch for a Social History of Post-Medieval Latin

The importance of Latin in the learned culture of medieval Europe is well known. After 1500, however, the story becomes more complicated. Did the Renaissance lead to the rise of Latin or the rise of the vernacular? Did Latin decline in the sixteenth century, the seventeenth, the eighteenth, the nineteenth or only in the twentieth? Posed in this simple form, the questions are imposs-ible to answer. They need rephrasing in the language of the sociolinguists, some of whom are currently preoccupied with language spread, language maintenance, language shift and language recession.[1]

The advantage of drawing on sociolinguistic theory is that it helps us to discriminate not only between, different parts of Europe and different kinds of Latin (classical and non-classical, spoken and written), but also between different kinds of user (clerical and lay, male and female, and so on), and between different topics or, to use the technical term, linguistic 'domains'.[2] The 'diglossia' or linguistic division of labour between Latin and the vernacular in early modern Europe was not so different from that between classical and vernacular forms of Arabic as analysed by contemporary sociolinguists.[3]

---

[1] Fishman (1972), 76–134; Cooper (1982); Wardhaugh (1987).
[2] Fishman (1965).
[3] Ferguson (1959). The relevance of the concept diglossia to studies of the relation between Latin and the vernacular was pointed out by Tavoni (1985), 484.

If these discriminations are made, it should become clear that Latin remained a living language in a number of situations as late as the nineteenth century. Such is the argument of this chapter, which is divided into three main sections, corresponding to the three main linguistic domains in which Latin was employed; the ecclesiastical, the academic, and the pragmatic.

If it were only possible, this study of 'post-medieval' Latin would take the Middle Ages as a base-line from which to measure change. However, as students of modern 'secularization' or 'dechristianization' have already discovered, it is exceedingly problematic to work with a base-line which encompasses about a thousand years. As an Italian scholar recently remarked, 'Medieval Latin is one, but it is not monolithic.'[4] For example, Latin was used much more widely in thirteenth-century lay society in Italy than it was in (say) England.[5] Unfortunately, there is no general history of the uses of Latin in the Middle Ages. The most that can be done here is to invoke the later Middle Ages from time to time in specific contexts.[6]

Still less work has been done on the post-medieval period in any of the three domains to be studied below. All this essay can hope to do is to offer examples which conflict with the conventional picture of the triumph of the vernacular in the seventeenth century (if not the sixteenth), and to draw a few provisional conclusions, which might be summed up in the form of three paradoxes, as follows.

1  The Protestants who were committed to the rejection of Latin in the church were often better Latinists than the Catholics who were committed to maintaining it.
2  A distinguished classical scholar once claimed that 'the Latin language was buried by humanism' ('durch den Humanismus die lateinische Sprache zu grabe getragen würde').[7] In other words, the decline of Latin was mainly due not to the oppo-

---

[4]  Feo (1986), 349.
[5]  Holmes (1986), 72–3.
[6]  Meillet (1928) is the work of a great linguist but ends long before the period discussed in this essay. Manitius (1911–31) is a magisterial work, but concerned only with literature. There is an important cluster of studies of early medieval Latin, including Lot (1931); Jackson (1948); Gratwick (1982); Richter (1983). More general contributions include Lehmann (1929); Coulton (1940); Norberg (1975–6); Sheerin (1987).
[7]  Norden (1898), 773.

nents of classical antiquity but to its supporters, the humanists, whose insistence on classical standards turned it from a living to a 'dead' language.

3  Although declared 'dead', Latin would not lie down. It remained useful, indeed vigorous in particular domains and in particular parts of Europe throughout the eighteenth and nineteenth centuries.


### ECCLESIASTICAL LATIN

Latin has been the official language of the Roman Catholic church for most of its history, not only for the liturgy (replacing Greek in the fourth century AD), but as the language of papal government, ecclesiastical courts, episcopal visitations, provincial synods, general councils, and other church business.[8] The encyclical letters from the popes to the faithful were and are written in Latin, as their titles remind us (*Rerum Novarum, Quadragesimo Anno,* etc.). The proceedings of Vatican II (*Acta Synodalia Concilii Oecumenici Vaticani II*) were published in Latin between 1970 and 1980.

Social historians must of course be attentive to the distance between the official and the unofficial. It may have been the case that the clergy who attended provincial synods employed the vernacular for their discussions, although the decrees which emerged were recorded in Latin. After all, many fifteenth- and sixteenth-century sermons by so-called popular preachers such as Gabriele Barletta and Olivier Maillard were published in Latin, when they must have been delivered in the vernacular. On the other hand, it is unlikely that masses were said in anything but Latin, or that the bishops from different parts of Europe assembled at general councils could have communicated in any other way.

More than one explanation can be offered for the persistence of Latin in this domain. In the first place, an international language was a valuable resource for an international organization (which in turn helped establish and maintain Latin as an international language). In the second place, the use of a non-vernacular langu-

---

[8]  The only general survey of this area known to me is Richter (1975). However, the Latin of early Christianity has been studied from a sociolinguistic point of view by Schrijnen (1932) and by his pupil Mohrmann (1958–61).

age acted as a marker, underlining the special nature of texts such as the Bible and rituals such as the Mass.[9] The controversy following the introduction of a vernacular liturgy (or more exactly, allowing it at the bishop's discretion) after Vatican II revealed the strength of the attachment to Latin, at least in some parts of Catholic Europe. Catholics are not of course the only religious group to use a 'dead' language as their language of spiritual power; the Hindus, Buddhists, Jews and Muslims, for example, employ Sanskrit, Pali, classical Hebrew and classical Arabic in a similar manner.[10]

Equally obvious, however, (at least to us) are the disadvantages of attempting to communicate with the whole population of Christendom in a language understood only by a relatively small minority of that population. Some of the laity believed that the use of Latin was a clerical trick to keep the faith secret, 'then sell it back to us retail' ('le vendono a poco a poco, come si dice a minuto').[11] It should be emphasized, however, that the minority who understood Latin excluded many of the medieval clergy. It is not surprising to learn that many of the parish clergy were ignorant of Latin, given the lack of facilities for training them, but even in the case of the monks, according to a well-known medievalist, 'we find the authorities assuming a great deal of Latin ignorance, and making special translations for the use of ignorant brethren.'[12]

Criticisms of the preponderance of Latin in the church were in fact made from time to time in the later Middle Ages, notably by the Waldensians and the Wyclifites, who insisted on having vernacular versions of the scriptures. These criticisms were made still more vigorously in the early sixteenth century. Erasmus, for example, appealed in his *Paraclesis* (1516) for the translation of the Bible into the vernacular:

I would that even the lowliest women read the Gospels and the Pauline Epistles. And I would that they were translated into all languages so that they could be read and understood not only by

[9] Mohrmann (1957), 12, 26.
[10] Tambiah (1968), esp. 23ff.; the statements about Latin are not altogether accurate, but the comparative analysis is enlightening.
[11] Gelli (1967), 69; cf. Gaetano (1976).
[12] Coulton (1940), 27.

Scots and Irish but also by Turks and Saracens ... Would that, as
a result, the farmer sing some portion of them at the plough, the
weaver hum some parts of them to the movement of his shuttle,
the traveller lighten the weariness of the journey with stories of
this kind.[13]

The irony of the situation is that Erasmus made this appeal in
Latin, and had to do so in order to be heard. Heard he was, but
not heeded; the Council of Trent outlawed the vernacular bibles
which had been circulating in the Catholic world from the late
Middle Ages, but were now associated with heresy.

As for the liturgy, in 1513 the Venetian hermits Paolo Giustiniani and Vincenzo Querini wrote to the Pope in favour of the
vernacular, and this proposal was discussed at the Council of
Trent and supported by the cardinal of Lorraine and the French
bishops.[14] Since liturgies had been devised in Greek, Coptic and
Church Slavonic earlier in the history of the church, this suggestion
did not breach any principle. All the same, and despite the felt
need to win back recent converts to Protestantism, the proposal
was unsuccessful so far as Europe was concerned. After a long
debate in which some leading clerics argued in favour of the
vernacular, the Council of Trent finally declared in 1562 that 'If
anyone should say ... that Mass should be celebrated in the
vernacular ... let him be anathema' ('Si quis dixerit ... lingua
tantum vulgari missum celebrari debere ... anathema sit').[15] In
the later sixteenth century, the Scuole della Dottrina Christiana,
organized to give the children of the poor an elementary knowledge
of theology and literacy, taught the *Ave Maria*, the *Credo*, the
*Pater Noster* and the *Salve Regina* in Latin, not Italian, as we
learn from the printed *Summario* distributed to the children.[16]

In practice, concessions were made. Following the Council of
Brest-Litovsk, at which the representatives of the Orthodox church
in the kingdom of Poland-Lithuania agreed to accept papal sup-
remacy if they could retain their own customs, Catholic services
in Old Church Slavonic could be heard. In East-Central Europe,

[13]   Translated in Olin (1965), 97.
[14]   V. Querini and P. Giustiniani, 'Libellus', in Mittarelli (1755–73), vol. 9, 681ff. Cf.
Travi (1984), esp. 52ff.
[15]   Quoted in Feo (1986), 369. On the debates, Lentner (1964), ch. 5; Coletti (1983).
[16]   Grendler (1984).

the bishops showed some sympathy for local vernaculars. In the diocese of Esztergom, for example, Hungarian German and Slovak as well as Latin could be used for baptisms and marriage services.[17] In the mission field outside Europe, concessions were also made on occasion. The Council of Lima, for example, decreed in 1582 that the Indians (unlike the Italian pupils of the Scuole della Dottrina Christiana) should not be forced to learn prayers or the catechism in Latin.[18] In 1615 the Chinese and in 1631 the Persians were granted the privilege of a liturgy in a language other than Latin (in Mandarin in one case, in classical Arabic in the other).

Sermons to the laity were generally in the vernacular. When San Carlo Borromeo criticized his episcopal colleague Gabriele Paleotti for preaching in Latin, Paleotti explained that his sermon had been addressed to the magistrates and doctors sitting near the high altar, while the rest of the people in the body of the church would have been unable to hear him.[19] In the case of French episcopal visitations, a shift from Latin to French took place in the course of the sixteenth and seventeenth centuries.[20] In these cases, the introduction of the vernacular did not carry the dangerous implication that the Protestants had been right all the time.

In any case, the simple contrast associating Catholicism with Latin and Protestantism with the vernacular is in need of qualification from the Protestant as well as the Catholic side. In the early years of Protestantism, the reformed liturgy was a Latin one. Even Luther's *German Mass*, issued in 1526, was intended for Sundays only, with a Latin liturgy continuing to be used on weekdays. Luther, Melanchthon and Zwingli wrote in Latin as well as in German, Calvin in Latin as well as in French. Indeed, of Calvin's 130 works, 79 were written in Latin.[21]

Like Erasmus, these reformers were caught in a dilemma. To write in Latin was to cut themselves off from ordinary people, but to write in a vernacular was to cut themselves off from the rest of Europe. Since the mother tongue of Erasmus was spoken

---

[17]  Béranger (1969), 14, citing the *Rituale Strigoniense* (1625).
[18]  Saenz (1755), vol. 4, 235. The decree itself was in Latin. On the use of Quechua by the church in Peru, see Heath and Laprade (1982).
[19]  Coletti (1983), 218.
[20]  Venard (1985), 52.
[21]  Calvin (1863–1900). Like others in the series Corpus Reformatorum, this collection was edited in Latin.

by relatively few people, it is scarcely surprising to find that he opted for Latin, in his three thousand private letters as well as in his voluminous works, and is recorded to have spoken his native language only on his deathbed. His last words were 'Lieve God' (Dear God). Before this he had been groaning in Latin, 'O Jesu, misericordia' and so on.[22]

The Protestant reformers, on the other hand, tended to prefer a bilingual compromise, switching from the vernacular to Latin according to the topic and the audience, and translating themselves or having themselves translated into Latin on occasion, as in the case of Luther's famous pamphlets *The Freedom of a Christian* and *The Babylonish Captivity of the Church*. This compromise worked all the better because – another irony – the sixteenth-century Protestant clergy, many of whom had attended university, were probably more competent in Latin than their Catholic colleagues. So far as the liturgy is concerned, the difference between the Protestant and the Catholic positions has been summed up as 'an evolution in opposite directions', as the reformers came to see the problems involved in abandoning Latin, and the Catholics those entailed by retaining it.[23]

## ACADEMIC LATIN

The importance of Latin literature in the sixteenth and seventeenth centuries – and even later – has been emphasized in recent studies, so there is little need to discuss it at length in this place.[24] Some earlier humanists were hostile to the use of the vernacular in literature – Giovanni del Virgilio, for example, who advised Dante to write his *Divine Comedy* in Latin.[25] A number of leading sixteenth-century humanists wrote treatises in defence of Latin, notably Romolo Amaseo, *De latinae linguae uso retinendi* (1529); Carlo Sigonio, *De latinae linguae uso retinendi* (1566); and Uberto Foglietta, *De linguae latinae praestantia* (1574).[26]

[22]  Huizinga (1924), 187.
[23]  Schmidt (1950), esp. 170.
[24]  For a survey with a full bibliography, see Ijsewijn (1977), 93–108. Cf. Ijsewijn (1987).
[25]  Feo (1986), 311–12. Klein (1957) surveys attitudes to the question from Dante to Manzoni.
[26]  Tavoni (1985).

Latin was employed in lyric and epic, poetry and prose, fiction and non-fiction. In the fifteenth century the leading Latin poets included Mantuanus, Pontano and Sannazzaro, all active in Italy; in the sixteenth century, the German humanist Conrad Celtis, the Pole Clemens Janicius (Janicki), and the Netherlander Johannes Secundus, famous for his 'Kisses' (*Basia*) first published in 1541; and in the seventeenth century, Milton and two Jesuits, the Italian Famiano Strada and the 'Polish Horace', Maciej Kazimierz Sarbiewski. In France too, Latin poetry continued to flourish in the early part of the reign of Louis XIV.[27] In the eighteenth century, no fewer than nine poems on Newton's system of the universe were published in Latin, one of them by the leading Jesuit astronomer Ruggiero Boscovitch.[28] As late as the nineteenth century, first-rate poetry was being written in Latin, notably by Giovanni Pascoli (who died in 1912). Pope Leo XIII was also an accomplished Latin poet.[29]

In the case of prose, it is perhaps worth stressing the survival of imaginative literature in Latin into the seventeenth and eighteenth centuries. Obvious examples are John Barclay's political *roman à clef*, the *Argenis* (1621), and Ludvig Holberg's satirical novel on the adventures of Niels Klimt underground, *N. Klimii Iter Subterraneum* (1741). As for the drama, its association with the teaching of Latin ensured a steady flow of plays throughout the sixteenth and seventeenth centuries, in particular in Jesuit colleges.[30]

However, the importance of Latin in post-medieval European culture is illustrated still more vividly by the large number of translations into that language made in the early modern period – more than 528 of them published between 1485 and 1799.[31]

Among the late medieval vernacular texts which were latinized in this period were Chaucer's *Troilus and Cressida*, Boccaccio's *Decameron*, Froissart's *Chronicles* and Marco Polo's accounts of his travels. A number of the famous vernacular texts of Renaissance Italy were also 'popularized' in this way, including Aretino's *Dialogues*, Machiavelli's *Prince*, Guicciardini's *History of Italy*,

[27] Vissac (1862).
[28] Naiden (1952).
[29] Traina (1971).
[30] Valentin (1978).
[31] Grant (1954); cf. Burke (c.1993a) and for Britain, Binns (1990), ch. 14.

Giovanni Della Casa's *Galateo*, and two of Ariosto's plays, while no fewer than three Latin versions of Castiglione's *Courtier* (or part of it) appeared in the course of the sixteenth century. Translations from Spanish into Latin included versions of Guevara's *Dial of Princes*, Alemán's novel *Guzmán de Alfarache* and Huarte's treatise on psychology, *Examen des ingénios*. Translations from French included the political writers Commynes, Seyssel and Bodin, as well as some of Ronsard's poems; translations from German, Brant's *Ship of Fools* and the travels of Heinrich von Staden; and translations from English, Spenser's *Shepherd's Calendar*. At least 166 vernacular texts were published in Latin translation in the course of the sixteenth century.

Translations of this kind were even more important in the seventeenth century, when at least 312 were published. In the early seventeenth century, the field was dominated by works of counter-reformation piety, generally written in Italian or Spanish, translated by Germans, and published in Cologne for the sake of northern European Catholics. The translations also included works by Arnauld (the *Logic* of Port-Royal), Bacon (the *Essays*), Boileau (the *Lutrin* and the ode on the capture of Namur), Descartes (the *Discours de la méthode* and the *Passions de l'âme*), Galileo (the *Letter to the Grand Duchess*), Hobbes (*Leviathan*), Locke (*Concerning Human Understanding*), Malebranche (*La recherche de la vérité*), Pascal (notably the *Lettres provinciales*), the *History of the Council of Trent* by Paolo Sarpi, and even the *History of the Reformation* by Gilbert Burnet, first published in 1679.

In the eighteenth century, the list of books translated into Latin fell sharply to 69 texts, which run from Gray's *Elegy* (in three independent versions) to the philosophical works of Kant. However, the fact that we still call the Chinese philosopher K'ung Fu Tzu 'Confucius' is a reminder that knowledge of his writings were spread in Europe from the late seventeenth century onwards in a Latin translation by a group of Jesuits.

Until the late seventeenth century, if not the early eighteenth, it remained more common for works of learning to be published in Latin than in any vernacular, even French. Descartes's *Discours de la méthode* has won him a distinguished place in the history of the 'rise' or 'emancipation' of French, so it is worth emphasizing the fact that he produced some of his books, such as his *Meditations*, in Latin. So did Francis Bacon, Thomas Hobbes (*De cive*, for example), John Locke and Isaac Newton. Galileo chose the vernacular from 1612 onwards because he wanted 'everyone' to be able to read about his discoveries and opinions, thus evoking protests from foreign acquaintances such as Mark Welser. However, his *Starry Messenger* and other works had been written in Latin.[32]

Even the vindications of their native tongues produced in the seventeenth century by the German poet Martin Opitz and the Czech Jesuit Bohuslav Balbín were themselves written in Latin, whether to reach an international public or because the dignity of the subject required it. To these examples could be added one still more famous, Dante's *De vulgari eloquentia*, but in this case the use of Latin had the advantage of not prejudging the issue, which kind of Italian to use.[33]

It has been argued that the middle of the seventeenth century was the turning point from Latin to the vernacular in France, the early eighteenth century for Germany. In the case of France, the evidence comes from the contents of libraries; in the case of Germany, from the books displayed for sale at the annual Frankfurt and Leipzig Book Fairs. At Leipzig in 1701, 55 per cent of the works displayed were in Latin; by 1740 the proportion had shrunk to 27 per cent.[34] The foundation of the *Journal des Savants*, the *Nouvelles de la République des Lettres* and other learned journals of the later seventeenth century did a good deal to establish French as the new language of the commonwealth of learning.

A good deal, but not quite enough. One of the most important international scholarly journals was the *Acta Eruditorum* of Leipzig, which began to appear in 1682 and utilized Latin, even when reviewing books in the vernacular such as Bayle on comets, or Bossuet on universal history. Its Swedish imitation, the *Acta Literaria Sueciae*, founded in 1720, followed the same policy, doubtless to acquire an international readership. When the Academy of St Petersburg began to publish its proceedings in 1720s, it too utilized Latin and they appeared as the *Commentarii Academiae Scientiarum Imperialis Petropolitanae*. As late as the mid-eighteenth century scholars can still be found who read little

[32] Migliorini (1960), 432ff.
[33] Opitz (1617); Balbín (1775). Cf. Kühlmann (1985).
[34] Martin (1969), 598; Goldfriedrich (1908), 69.

that was not in Latin – Vico, for example. Although he decided
to write his *New Science* in Italian, his earlier works had been in
Latin. Vico's lament, in a letter of 1726, over the fall in the
price of Latin books in Naples as a result of declining demand is
often quoted.[35]

By the eighteenth century such attitudes were old-fashioned,
and the victory of the vernaculars was unquestionable. The French
journalist Jacques Vincent Delacroix was cruelly correct when he
wrote in the 1770s comparing Latin to a house 'richement meublée,
spacieuse et abandonée'.[36] Yet the defeat of Latin was not complete, and it may be worth emphasizing how late learned works
continued to be written in that language.[37] The Swiss mathematician Jakob Bernoulli I published his *Ars conjectandi* in that
language in 1713. Later in the eighteenth century, his compatriot
Leonhard Euler published his *Mechanica* (1736) and his *Intro-
ductio in analysin infinitorum* (1748), although he also wrote in
French and German. As late as the middle of the nineteenth
century, the German mathematician Carl Friedrich Gauss was
publishing his work in Latin.

Mathematicians were not alone in this respect. Some academic
traditions positively required Latin publications. In nineteenth-
century France, the supplementary thesis for the doctorate of
letters had to be written in Latin, whether the subject was the
poetry of Keats (A.-J. Angellier, *De Joh. Keatsii vita et carminibus*,
1892), the criminal jurisdiction of the Paris Châtelet (L.-J. Batiffol,
*De castelleto parisiensi circa 1400 annum et qua ratione crimi-
nales judicaverit*, 1896), the fiscal policies of Louis XVI (P. Sagnac,
*Quomodo jura dominii aucta fuerint regnante Ludovico Sexto
Decimo*, 1898), or the development of sociological method
(C. Bouglé, *Quid e Cournoti disciplina ad scientias 'sociologicas'
promovendas sumere liceat*, 1899), despite the need for neologisms
such as *scientiae 'sociologicae'*. The authors of such published
theses included Henri Bergson (*Quid Aristotles de loco senserit*,
1889); E. J. Renan (*De philosophia peripatetica*, 1852); Charles
Seignebos (*De indole plebis romanae apud Titum Livium*, 1882);
and perhaps the most famous of all, E. Durkheim (*Quid Secun-
datus politicae scientiae instituendae contulerit*, 1892). It would

35  Vico (1929), 207.
36  Delacroix (1770–1).
37  Cf. Basile (1984).

be interesting to know whether these Latin theses were entirely
the work of their authors, or whether there was some kind of
unofficial translation service available. Specialists in the writing
of Latin dissertations could be found in some universities in the
Netherlands in the nineteenth century.[38]

Academic Latin was not only a written but also a spoken
language. It is well known that university lectures and disputations
took place in that language, while many schools not only taught
Latin but taught in Latin, and insisted that the pupils speak Latin
even in the playground. What is difficult is to distinguish between
theory and practice, to chart regional and other variations in that
practice and to date changes, all this on the basis of written
sources. The examples which follow are not claimed to be typical;
they are offered simply in order to show the difficulty of generalization, and to encourage more systematic research in this area.

In the case of schools, there is little doubt that proficiency in
spoken Latin was frequently required from the pupils, under-
standably so given Latin's practical value (to be discussed in the
following section of this essay). Hence the importance of printed
dialogues for use in schools, notably those of Erasmus and Cor-
dier; the study of the plays of Plautus and Terence (despite
suspicion of their immorality); the rise of the so-called 'school
drama', in other words the regular performance of Latin plays by
schoolboys; and the institution of the *lupus*, the 'wolf' or spy
who was supposed to inform the teacher if he heard his comrades
speak in the vernacular during playtime. Montaigne and Roberto
Gentili were exceptional in being taught Latin as their first language, but these exceptions should be seen as an extreme case of a
general insistence that upper-class children come early to Latin.

It may still be something of a shock to pick up one of the most
famous Latin grammars of the Renaissance, Lorenzo Valla's
*Elegantiae linguae latinae*, and to discover that it is written throughout in Latin, so that it cannot be understood without a knowledge
of the language it claims to impart. The prevalence of Latin
grammars in Latin has led one historian of education to comment
on the importance of the 'direct method' in Renaissance education.[39] He may be right. A remarkable and relatively well-docu-

---

[38] Bergmann (1988), 96ff.
[39] Ong (1958), 11.

mented example of this approach, giving ability to converse priority over grammar, is that of the Flemish humanist Nicolas Clenardus, who taught in Portugal, experimenting with his new method on three black slaves before introducing it to his classes.[40]

However, we should not jump to conclusions about teaching methods in the Renaissance. We do not know whether Valla's book was generally used as a manual for the student or only for the teacher, or whether many sixteenth-century teachers mixed explanation in the vernacular with their official insistence on spoken Latin.

In any case, there is evidence of increasing dissatisfaction with the monopoly of Latin in the classroom, at least from the seventeenth century onwards, from the *Janua linguarum* (1631) of Jan Amos Comenius – yet another critique of Latin in Latin – to Jean-Baptiste de la Salle. In eighteenth-century German schools, at least 'some of the explanations required in Latin classes were given in German'.[41] Yet teaching children to read in Latin remained normal practice in France until the 1870s and survived in some places until the twentieth century.[42]

In the case of universities, there is a little more information available about variations and changes in practice. Spoken Latin was the norm in early modern Europe, as far east as the Theological Academy of Kiev in the early seventeenth century, where Peter Mogila, who opposed the union with Rome, wanted his students to understand the enemy.[43] All the same, some teachers employed the vernacular themselves or allowed their students to do so. Antonio Genovesi, in 1765, claimed to be the first professor to teach philosophy in Italian at the University of Naples (what would Vico have thought?) but this was not the first time Italian had been heard in lectures in the peninsula.[44] In the law faculty of the University of Rome in the sixteenth century, Latin was the language most commonly used for the disputations, but provision was made for the use of Italian in case of difficulties.[45]

In the Netherlands in the later sixteenth century, the mathe-

---

[40] Watson (1915), esp. 131–2.
[41] La Vopa (1988), 63; cf. Gessinger (1980), 65–79.
[42] Brunot (1905–), vol. 5, 39n.
[43] Zernov (1961), 148.
[44] Genovesi (1775), vol. 2, 51–2.
[45] Conte (1985), 81.

matician Simon Stevin taught in Dutch.[46] In Paris at about the
same time, Louis Le Roy, who taught politics, gave some of his
lectures in French.[47] An English student of medicine, Edward
Browne (son of the famous Sir Thomas) went to Paris in 1664
and attended the lectures of Guy Patin, 'but I was much disap-
pointed in my expectation of understanding all hee said by reason
hee used the French tongue so much'.[48] At Montpellier a few
years later, John Locke attended a disputation in the Faculty of
Medicine; his laconic comment was 'hard Latin' and 'Much
French.'[49] At the Collège Royal in Paris, lectures in French law in
French were given by Professor Delaunay in 1680 (though he was
criticized at the time for doing so).[50]

Exceptions to the Latin rule can also be found in the German-
speaking world. As early as 1501, the humanist Heverlingh lectured
on Juvenal in German at the University of Rostock. Paracelsus
delivered his notorious lectures in Basle in 1526–7 in German,
before he was asked to leave, and one wonders whether the
untraditional medium was not considered as offensive as the
unorthodox message. However, Christian Thomasius seems 'to
have been the first person to announce a course of lectures in
German', a course on the ethics of the Spanish writer Baltasar
Gracián, delivered at the University of Halle in 1687.[51] He was
followed by A. H. Francke at Leipzig.

In Britain too we can find exceptions to the rule of Latin. In
the early seventeenth century, English was used as well as Latin
in the lectures at Gresham College, Latin for the sake of foreign
listeners and English because, as Sir Thomas Gresham put it in
his will, 'the greatest part of the auditory is like to be of such
citizens and others as have small knowledge, or none at all, in the
Latin tongue.'[52] John Webster's criticism of the universities of
Oxford and Cambridge, in his *Academiarum Examen* (1654), for
teaching in Latin seems to have been little heeded in his own
time. Indeed, a few years later, the president and fellows of
Queens' College Cambridge enjoined the undergraduates to speak

[46] Branden (1956), 77.
[47] Ong (1958), 13.
[48] Browne (1923), 3–4.
[49] Locke (1953), 50.
[50] Brunot (1905–), vol. 5, 59.
[51] Blackall (1959), 12.
[52] Cited in Hill (1965), 34–5.

Latin in hall at dinner and supper.[53] In Harvard College in the seventeenth century, the use of English was prohibited within the college precincts.[54] Speaking Latin was a sign of a student, and apparently sufficient to lead to brawling in the streets and even to homicide, at least in northern France in the sixteenth and seventeenth centuries.[55]

In the early eighteenth century, on the other hand, a Danish student at Oxford (later to become a famous man of letters) reported that although he spoke Latin 'with difficulty and hesitation', he found that 'the English admired the readiness and fluency with which I expressed myself in that language. The truth is, that this exercise is so neglected in England that I met with no one, except Dr Smalridge, who could speak Latin tolerably.'[56] In Scotland it seems that the eighteenth century was the turning point from Latin to the vernacular. The philosopher Frances Hutcheson is said to have been the first professor at Glasgow to lecture in English, though even he had given his inaugural in Latin in 1730.

In some parts of Europe, however, Latin persisted into the nineteenth century as the language of teaching. The advocate George Bergmann (1805–92), who studied at Leiden and Ghent, recalled oral examinations in Latin. Gauss was still lecturing in Latin at Göttingen in the middle of the nineteenth century, while Jean Charles Naber is supposed to have lectured on Roman law in Latin at the University of Utrecht as late as 1911.[57]

On special occasions Latin lasted even longer, perhaps to give these occasions added solemnity, to show that they were in some sense sacred. Inaugural lectures, for example, continued to be given in Latin in the nineteenth century. Thus Ranke gave his inaugural lecture at Berlin in 1836 on the knowledge of and the distinction between history and politics, ('De historiae et politicae cognitione atque discrimine'), complaining while he was preparing it that 'Unfortunately a Latin dissertation and lecture are still required, which I have little desire to do.'[58] At the University of

[53]   Twigg (1987), 217.
[54]   Morison (1936), 84.
[55]   Lille, Archives Départementales du Nord, B 1751, f.39, B 1766, f.188, B 1801, f.143. I owe all these references to the kindness of Robert Muchembled.
[56]   Holberg (1970), 43. Holberg was at Oxford 1706–8.
[57]   Bergmann (1988), 96–101; Gerbenzon (1987).
[58]   Quoted in Wines (1981), 106.

Leiden in 1850, a distinguished Arabist, Dozy, gave offence (to the curators, at least) by lecturing in Dutch at his inauguration instead of in Latin. In Cambridge, Latin remained the language of the Harveian orations until the late nineteenth century, leading to at least one acutely embarrassing occasion remembered by Lord Moran as 'that dreadful day in October, 1864, when Robert Lee began the Harveian Oration in Latin, and had perforce to finish it in his own tongue'.[59] Latin remains to this day the language of the panegyrics on honorary doctorands delivered by the public orator on degree days in Oxford, Cambridge, and some traditional continental universities such as Lund.

In any case, until the early twentieth century it was possible to assume that educated Europeans had at least an elementary knowledge of Latin, while other people did not. Hence the employment of Latin as a cipher by middle-class whites in Africa in one of the novels of John Buchan, *Prester John* (1910).

## PRAGMATIC LATIN

I have coined the phrase 'pragmatic Latin' to refer to a variety of practical uses for that language, usually in international contexts such as diplomacy and travel, but also in that of the law, and even of business on occasion. As late as the 1870s some Oxford colleges, such as Lincoln and Merton, were keeping their accounts in Latin.[60]

To a greater or lesser extent Latin was used as the language of the law all over Europe. As terms like habeas corpus remind us, it was even employed in regions such as England where the influence of Roman law was relatively slight. Early in the English civil war the Commission of Array, calling out the militia to fight for the king, was in Latin, with the result that in Somerset the king's opponents 'translated it into what English they pleased'.[61] In some parts of early modern Europe there was a revolt against lawyers' Latin. In 1534, for example, the Polish gentry criticized its use at the Dietine or local assembly held at Sroda, while in 1539, in the famous ordinance of Villers-Cottêrets, François I

---

[59] Quoted in Newman (1957), 50–1.
[60] Green (1979), 492.
[61] Clarendon (1888), vol. 2, 296.

ordered French to be used in legal documents.[62] Similar demands were made by radicals, such as John Jones, during the English Revolution.[63]

The criticism of legal Latin was probably strongest in Italy, despite or because of the fact that the law was even more involved with Latin there than elsewhere. In 1444, for example, the people of Curzola complained that the 'gentlemen' were exploiting their knowledge of Latin to the disadvantage of ordinary people (the *popolari*).[64] Carlo Ginzburg's Menocchio was not alone in denouncing the use of Latin in court as 'treason to the poor' ('un tradimento de'poveri').[65] The parallel with Gelli's critique of church Latin (discussed above) is an obvious one, and it is interesting to find that Paolo Giustiniani and Vincenzo Querini advocated the use of Italian in notarial documents as well as in the Mass. However, legal Latin survived in the states of the church until the revolution of 1831.[66]

Latin was on occasion the language of domestic politics. There is at least one example of a chief minister speaking Latin to his sovereign: Sir Robert Walpole to George I. His son Horace recalled that 'Sir Robert governed George 1st in Latin, the King not speaking English, and his Minister no German, nor even French. It was much talked of, that Sir Robert detecting one of the Hanoverian Ministers in some trick or falsehood before the King's face, had the firmness to say to the German, *Mentiris impudentissime!*'[67]

The best-known case of the domestic use of Latin, however, is that of the Hungarian Diet. Its *Acta* were recorded in Latin and it is likely that that language was used for most of the speeches, since speakers of Hungarian, Croat and Slovak would not otherwise have been able to communicate with one another. Latin was also used for many official communications in the Holy Roman Empire, whether for practical or symbolic reasons. The Austrian monarchy also used Latin for convenience to communicate with Hungary and Slovakia (which were outside the empire). The

---

[62] Isambert (1827–33), vol. 12, 592ff.
[63] Quoted by Hill (1965), 261.
[64] Cozzi (1980), 74ff.
[65] Ginzburg (1976), 9. Curiously enough, Alessandro Manzoni makes his hero the peasant Renzo utter similar sentiments in his novel *I promessi sposi*, ch. 2.
[66] Feo (1986), 372.
[67] Walpole (1924), 14–15. However, Hatton (1978), 129ff., claims that the king did know some English.

financial officials of the Hofkammer in Vienna, for example, corresponded in Latin with their counterparts in Bratislava. The Emperor Joseph II decided that German should be the language of administration, telling the Hungarians in 1784, in true enlightened-despotic style, that a dead language could not reasonably be used for official purposes. The nobility disliked the change, associating Latin with liberty, and in the 1790s Leopold brought it back. Latin remained the official language of the kingdom of Hungary until 1844.[68]

It was, however, in international relations that Latin, spoken and written, really came into its own, remaining important all over Europe throughout the sixteenth and seventeenth centuries and surviving considerably longer in some areas. In the days when the news appeared in annual volumes rather than weekly or daily, one of the best-known series appeared in Latin: the *Mercurius Gallobelgicus*, published at Cologne and Frankfurt between 1594 and 1630.

No wonder there was a demand for Latin secretaries to princes, not only in the Renaissance when Budé served François I and Ammonio, Henry VIII, but well into the seventeenth century. The English Commonwealth, for example, employed Georg Weckherlin, John Milton and Andrew Marvell in this capacity. Princes were not alone in their need for Latin secretaries. Archbishop Parker of Canterbury employed J. Joscelyn in this capacity from 1558 onwards.

George I is far from the only ruler recorded to have spoken Latin. The Emperor Maximilian prided himself on his knowledge of that language (and of a number of others).[69] Queen Elizabeth lost her temper in Latin on a famous occasion in 1597, when she considered herself insulted by the Polish ambassador.[70] On a more friendly occasion, in Copenhagen in 1634, Christian IV spoke Latin to the French ambassador d'Avaux, who had addressed him in Italian.[71] D'Avaux also spoke Latin to the eight-year-old Queen Christina of Sweden, or more exactly, spoke over her head to Salvius, who replied in the same language.[72]

It should not be assumed, however, that early modern diplomats

---

[68]  Béranger (1969).
[69]  Waas (1941), 34.
[70]  Stow (1601), 1299ff., gives a tactful account of the incident.
[71]  Ogier (1656), 52.
[72]  Ibid., 148, 150.

were fluent in Latin, only that they were expected to manage
somehow. George Downing was unusually frank but may not
have been otherwise exceptional when he confessed to secretary
Thurloe in 1655 that he had spoken 'as well as I could in Latin'
during a two-hour interview with Cardinal Mazarin.[73]

Latin was not the sole language of diplomacy in the seventeenth
century, but it certainly had its advantages. Treaties were commonly drafted in Latin in the sixteenth and seventeenth centuries;
the Peace of Westphalia of 1648, for example, published in 1651
as *Tractatus Pacis inter Hispaniam et Unitum Belgium Monasterii*.
Britain long continued to use Latin for international treaties, as
can be seen from a glance at those collected in Thomas Rymer's
*Foedera* (1704–32). And how else could a Portuguese (for
example) have communicated with a Swede? When Francisco
de Sousa Coutinho was ambassador to Stockholm in the seventeenth century, the communications of both sides were translated
into Latin.[74]

The advantages of Latin were symbolic as well as pragmatic,
as the Swedish chancellor, Axel Oxenstierna, explained to the
English ambassador, Bulstrode Whitelocke, in 1653: He spake
Latin, plain and fluent and significant; and

> though he could, yet would not speak French, saying he knew no
> reason why that nation should be so much honoured more than
> others as to have their language used by strangers; but he thought
> the Latin more honourable and more copious, and fitter to be
> used, because the Romans had been masters of so great a part of
> the world, and yet at present that language was not peculiar to
> any people.[75]

Whichever reasons were paramount, in some quarters Latin
was able to resist the rise of French as the language of diplomacy
in the reign of Louis XIV. Contrary to legend, both oral and
written Latin were employed as well as French in the negotiations
at Nijmegen leading to the peace treaty of 1679 between France
and her enemies (the Austrian Empire, Spain, and the United

[73]   Birch (1742), vol. 3, 734.
[74]   Ahnlund (1943), 116.
[75]   Whitelocke (1855), vol. 1, 300.

Provinces).[76] At Frankfurt in 1682, the Empire insisted on Latin, and France on French.[77] Treaties continued to be made in Latin much later, including those between England and Sweden in 1720 and between the Austrian Empire and Sweden in 1757. At the end of the nineteenth century, the Habsburg Emperor was still writing to the King of Sweden in Latin.[78]

In the reign of Louis XIV, a considerable effort was made by Colbert to project a favourable image of the king and his achievements, abroad as well as at home. To this end medals were struck to commemorate the major events of the reign, statues were erected and engravings of these statues were circulated. Voices were raised in favour of French as the language of the inscriptions, but in practice Latin was almost always used, despite the fact that the famous dispute between ancients and moderns was taking place at this time. Latin was still the only sure way to reach an international public.[79]

Private individuals also found Latin useful or even, on occasion, indispensable. As late as the mid-eighteenth century, Voltaire was conducting a small part of his international correspondence in Latin (though less than Italian or even English). English travellers abroad in the early modern period were more likely (like Sir Robert Walpole) to be fluent in Latin than in French, Italian, Spanish or German. Among those who recorded having spoken Latin in France and Italy are Thomas Coryat; Sir George Courthop, who conversed with a Jesuit in the famous convent of possessed nuns in Loudun; Peter Heylyn (who got lost in Paris and asked some priests the way); and John Locke (who failed to communicate in Lyons).[80] Gilbert Burnet, who knew Italian, was reduced to speaking Latin in Lombardy because he did not understand the local dialect.[81] Samuel Johnson was also, according to Boswell, 'very resolute in speaking Latin' in France, and according to Mrs Thrale conducted a long conversation in that language with an abbé in Rouen.[82]

---

[76]   Brunot (1905–), vol. 5, 402ff.
[77]   Ibid., 411ff.
[78]   Westrin (1900), 336, 338–9.
[79]   Le Laboureur (1667); Charpentier (1676). Cf. Brunot (1905–), vol. 5, 16–23; Magne (1976), 404ff., 483ff.; Beugnot (1979).
[80]   Lough (1984), 11, 12, 165, 198; Courthop (1907), 107; Locke (1953), 6.
[81]   Burnet (1686), 111.
[82]   Boswell (1934), vol. 2, 404; Piozzi (1974), 93–4.

Seventeenth-century French visitors to England found Latin equally useful, as two examples mentioned by John Evelyn suggest. When he introduced 'a young French Sorbonnist' to Jeremy Taylor, the two men began to argue in Latin about the problem of original sin. Similarly, the refugee Huguenot minister Pierre Allix found Latin the best means to communicate with the Archbishop of Canterbury.[83] Dr Johnson was perhaps a little old-fashioned in keeping up the Latin habit in the late eighteenth century. It is understandable that he should have spoken Latin with the Jesuit astronomer Ruggiero Boscovitch (a Croat who taught in Italy), but a little more surprising that when he was introduced to a distinguished Frenchman at the Royal Academy, 'he would not deign to speak French, but talked Latin, though his Excellency did not understand it, owing, perhaps, to Johnson's English pronunciation.'[84]

Yet Johnson was not the last Englishman to have recourse to Latin when confronted by foreigners. In our own century Hilaire Belloc, with a kind of Johnsonian perversity, insisted on speaking Latin in Italy, beginning a conversation with a priest in the village of Sillano, 'Pater, habeo linguam latinam, sed non habeo linguam italicam.'[85]

In an age when the Dutch were less proficient in English than they are now, it was only to be expected that Englishmen would speak Latin in the Netherlands, so that Sir Philip Sidney, for example, spoke Latin on his deathbed at Zutphen.[86] Again, Queen Elizabeth's extempore speech to the Polish ambassador in 1597 has its parallel in her conversation with a Spanish captain, Pedro Sarmiento de Gamboa, in 1586. 'He conversed with her in Latin for more than two hours and a half.' Sarmiento also conversed in Latin with Sir Walter Ralegh.[87] Examples of this kind could easily be multiplied.

It was above all in East-Central Europe that Latin came into its own as an indispensable lingua franca, as the example of the Hungarian Diet has already suggested. When Henri, Duc d'Anjou, went to Poland after his election as king of that country in 1573,

[83]  Evelyn (1955), vol. 3, 171, 288.
[84]  Boswell (1934), vol. 2, 125, 404, 406.
[85]  Belloc (1902), 372.
[86]  Sidney (1973), 171.
[87]  Markham (1895), 341–2.

the Frenchmen in his suite were surprised (and doubtless relieved) to discover that almost all the gentry, and 'all sorts of people, even the innkeepers' spoke Latin.[88] They obviously noticed a genuine difference between Poland and France, even if they exaggerated it. In 1643, a Spanish soldier found Latin useful in Warsaw (as I did myself in 1964, when I was lost and asked a priest the way).[89] A Polish gentleman of the mid-seventeenth century, Jan Pasek, on campaign in Denmark, tells us that he was posted to Jutland 'chiefly owing to my Latin', as if his comrades were unskilled in the language. He goes on to explain that 'the peasants there can speak Latin', probably another exaggeration, to judge from the lack of communication when he arrived.[90] Another witness to the Polish nobility's familiarity with Latin of some kind is the Duc de St-Simon, who noted that when the Poles entertained the Prince de Conti, 'they all spoke Latin, and very bad Latin at that' ('ils parlaient tous Latin, et fort mauvais Latin').[91] The evidence of Polish family letters points in the same direction.

The relative importance of Latin in eighteenth-century Finland might also be explained in practical terms as a lingua franca for a nation which could not reasonably expect foreigners to learn its language.[92] A similar point might be made about Iceland. A visitor to Reykjavik in 1856 discovered that 'Many of the inhabitants speak English, and one or two French, but in default of either of these, your only chance is Latin.' He also records going to a banquet where the speeches were in Latin.[93] In Hungary the situation was much the same. It is not at all uncommon to find Hungarians corresponding in Latin – some sort of Latin – in the sixteenth and seventeenth centuries.[94] They also spoke the language in everyday life. The physician Edward Browne (whom we have already encountered as a student in Paris) noted that 'The Latin-Tongue is very serviceable in Hungaria and Transylvania', where 'very great numbers' spoke it, 'especially the Gentry and Souldiers',

---

[88] Cimber and Danjou (1836), vol. 5, 142.
[89] Quoted in Braudel (1979), 165.
[90] Pasek (1929), 23–4.
[91] St-Simon (1983–), vol. 1, 406.
[92] Kajanto (1979).
[93] Dufferin (1903), 22, 39.
[94] Examples in Veres (1944). On the deficiencies of the Hungarian nobleman Ádám Batthyány's Latin letters to the Kriegshofrat in Vienna, Evans (1979), 259.

while even 'Coachmen, Watermen and mean Persons . . . could make themselves understood thereby.'[95]

That Browne was right, particularly about the soldiers, is suggested by an incident involving the future Maréchal de Bassompierre, who was on campaign against the Turks near Esztergom in 1603. Scouts were sent out to look for the enemy, and one of them, riding back at full speed, shouted to the foreigner, 'Heu domine, adsunt Turcae', 'Look out sir, the Turks are here!' In this case knowledge of Latin might be described as necessary for survival.[96]

## CONCLUSIONS

This brief survey of the uses of Latin in different linguistic domains raises a number of questions about the kind of Latin which was written and spoken in post-medieval Europe, and about the geography, sociology and chronology of its use. In the present state of knowledge it is impossible to do more than hint at the answers to these questions, but at this point it may be useful to define more precisely the major problems for future research.

It would, for example, be interesting to know more about the division of labour between Latin and vernacular, and the conscious and unconscious rules for switching codes. The exceptional case of Montaigne helps reveal the norm. Montaigne tells us that he was taught Latin as his first or 'natural' language, with the result that forty years later he would find himself reverting to it in the case of 'extrêmes et soudaines émotions'.[97] Normally, however even the most fluent Latin speaker and writer (Erasmus, for example, as his last words suggest) used Latin as a second language, while most users probably thought in the vernacular. It is likely that Coulton's comment on medieval Latinists remained true in the early modern period: 'In the inmost thoughts even of the most learned men, the mother-tongue seems always, or nearly always, to have remained uppermost.'[98] Even the encyclicals of the accomplished Latinist Leo XIII were drafted in Italian and

---

[95] Browne (1673), 13–14.
[96] Bassompierre (1665), 88.
[97] Montaigne (1588), 1.26, 3.2.
[98] Coulton (1940), 15.

translated into Latin by the Secretary of Latin Letters (although the Pope might extemporize alterations).[99] It has been plausibly argued that neo-Latin poets faced a serious problem when it came to expressing and communicating emotions, because they were writing in a language which for writer and reader alike was devoid of the associations of early childhood.[100]

It was examples like these which led me to formulate the second paradox above, to the effect that the decline of Latin was mainly due not to the opponents of classical antiquity but to its supporters, the humanists, whose insistence on classical standards turned it from a living to what Pietro Bembo called a 'dead' language. The statement may well be exaggerated. After all, insistence on standards of this kind has never been able to kill colloquial vernaculars such as French or English.

It should also be pointed out that some humanists at least were not afraid to modify classical usage when they thought it necessary. Ironically enough, the 'dead' language Latin had to be employed to express new ideas, because of the lack of abstract terms in most European vernaculars. The gradual rise of the vernaculars in the sixteenth and seventeenth centuries as the languages of scientific treatises was associated with their Latinization; new words had to be coined, and they were normally derived from Latin.[101]

The varieties of Latin employed in this period also deserve emphasis. One might start from the fact that different pronunciations of Latin sometimes made international communication problematic. The English pronunciation of Latin was (and perhaps still is) notoriously difficult for other Latinists to understand. Samuel Sorbière complained about this when he visited England in the middle of the seventeenth century.[102] So did the biblical scholar Samuel Bochart.[103] John Evelyn confirmed the justice of the complaint when he commented on the 'odd pronouncing of Latin' by his fellow-countrymen, 'so that out of England no nation were able to understand or endure it'.[104] So did Robert Samber, in the dedication to his new translation of Castiglione's

[99] Antoniazzi (1957).
[100] Spitzer (1955).
[101] On the lack of abstractions in Polish, Backvis (1958); on French, Febvre (1942), 384ff. On the Latinization of the vernacular, Johnson (1944).
[102] Quoted in Brunot (1905–), vol. 5, 390n.
[103] Bochart (1692), 3.
[104] Evelyn (1955), vol. 3, 288; cf. Lauder, quoted in Lough (1984), 12.

*Courtier*, in 1729: 'I have been told by several learned Foreigners in the most polite parts of Europe, that they are in pain when we speak Latin.'

The humanists of the Renaissance revived classical and especially Ciceronian Latin, and employed it not only for their literary works but also in the chanceries where some of them spent a good deal of their time. Some of them, Leonardo Bruni for example, obtained important posts in government on the basis of their proficiency in classical Latin.[105]

However, as humanist historians discovered, classical Latin was not altogether appropriate as a language for describing the post-classical world. How was one to describe new technology (such as gunpowder or the printing press), new institutions (such as the papacy), new religions (from Islam to Protestantism), or parts of the world unknown to the Romans (from China to Peru)? Some humanists solved the problem by classicizing the modern, calling the Pope 'pontifex maximus' (an ancient Roman title) or Lombardy 'Gallia Cisalpina'. Others were uncomfortable with this solution, whether, like Uberto Foglietta, they concluded that modern history should be written in the vernacular, or, like Hugo Grotius, they invented new terms like *Calvinistae* or *Protestantes*.[106]

Medieval Latin also survived the attacks of the humanists, in the church, in the universities and in the offices of many lawyers and notaries. In the case of the church, medieval and Renaissance Latin coexisted. For a sixteenth-century example of the clash between the two varieties we may turn to the text of the *Spiritual Exercises* of St Ignatius Loyola, which was 'translated' from Ignatius's own rather idiosyncratic Latin into a more classical form by the humanist-trained Jesuit André des Freux.[107] A more recent and highly controversial example is that of the new translation of the Psalter into classical (or at any rate classicizing) Latin commissioned by Pope Pius XII and completed in 1944, much criticized for its break with a long Christian tradition.[108]

In the universities, the survival and indeed the revival of scholastic philosophy in the sixteenth and seventeenth centuries meant

[105]  Rizzo (1986), 379.
[106]  Foglietta (1574), 15; Grotius (1657).
[107]  Ignatius (1963), 186.
[108]  Mohrmann (1958–61), vol. 2, 109–31.

that medieval Latin did not die out altogether. It is difficult not to sympathize with the lady who wrote to the *Leipzig Spectator* in 1723, saying that she loved philosophy but could not understand the 'Latin jargon' ('das rothwelsche Latein') in which it was discussed.[109]

Medieval Latin included not only post-classical terms but also constructions modelled on the vernacular. For example, the fifteenth-century Italian chronicler Stefano Infessura uses phrases which need to be translated back into Italian to become intelligible. His phrase for 'cheap' is *pro bono fora* (in Italian, *a buon mercato*), and for 'he stood up' he uses *erexit se in pedes* (in other words, *si levò in piedi*).[110]

It is this kind of 'coarse Latin' (*Latinus grossus*) which was parodied by the humanist monk Teofilo Folengo in poems such as the *Liber Macaronices* (1517), so called because it was written in 'macaronic Latin', as coarse as macaroni. In his mock-epic *Baldus*, for example, Folengo obtained some of his comic effects by coining non-classical terms for modern weapons; *alebardae* (halberds), *partesanae* (partesans), *picchiae* (pikes), *spontones* (spontoons) and so on.[111] Other humanists wrote macaronic prose, producing at least two masterpieces, the *Epistolae obscurorum virorum* and the *Passavant*. The latter text is a piece of anti-papal propaganda written in a truly Rabelaisian style, which describes Pope Julius III taking the work of an anti-Protestant propagandist to read in the lavatory, 'and when he wanted to wipe his behind with it, he found your style so rough that he took the skin off the apostolic seat' ('et ibi cum voluisset semel suas nates abstergere cum illo, reperit vestrum stilum tam durum, quod sibi decorticavit totam Sedem Apostolicam').[112]

Macaronic Latin was at once an object of satire, a symbol of the ignorance of the traditional clergy, and a medium of satire, close to the direct, colloquial, earthy vernacular.[113] These different types of vernacularized Latin are the inverse of the Latinized vernacular which was employed in certain circles in late medieval and early modern Europe.

[109]   *Der Leipzige Spectateur* (1723), 119.
[110]   Infessura (1890), xvii.
[111]   Paoli (1959).
[112]   Beza (1554), 37.
[113]   Hess (1971).

Along with this interaction and interpenetration of Latin and vernacular, it is hardly surprising to find examples of switching from one to the other. Latin documents such as contracts or interrogations may suddenly slip into the vernacular when some untranslatable technical term is needed. In the case of the contract between Domenico Ghirlandaio and Giovanni Tornabuoni, for example, for paintings in the church of Santa Maria Novella in Florence, it was laid down that the paintings were to be 'as they say in the vernacular, frescoed' ('ut vulgariter dicitur, posti in frescho').[114] Italian diocesan synods frequently slip into the vernacular to identify the popular practices which they were trying to reform; *vulgo cicale, vulgato nomine Nizzarda,* etc.[115]

The reverse process was also a common one. In both speech and writing there was a tendency to slip into Latin at certain points. Luther did this in his *Table-Talk,* and the records of the Swedish Riksdag of the seventeenth century, or indeed the English House of Commons, are also full of Latin phrases, like the following: 'As in *Corruptissima republica* there may be *plurimae leges,* so it is true, as the Bishop of Winchester said today in his sermon, *ex malis moribus bonae leges oriuntur.*'[116] Interrogations by inquisitors and other ecclesiastics were generally recorded in Latin, but the answers might be recorded in the vernacular. In fifteenth-century Italy, for example, or seventeenth-century Germany, letters in the vernacular might begin or end with Latin phrases, perhaps to give the text more dignity.[117] In a similar manner, Machiavelli employed Latin for the titles of the chapters in his *Prince.*[118] Again, the diarist Marino Sanudo regularly switched from his Venetian vernacular to Latin terms such as *licet, etiam, tamen, tunc, succincte, in sacris,* etc., and back again.[119]

This kind of switching may have been easier for Italians than for most Europeans, but it was certainly not confined to them. Another famous diarist who has already appeared in these pages, the seventeenth-century nobleman Jan Pasek, included many Latin

[114]  Milanesi (1901), 134ff.
[115]  Corrain and Zampini (1970), 43n. 235, etc.
[116]  Stolt (1964) compares Luther's practice with the Riksdag's; cf. Notestein (1935), vol. 2, 5–6.
[117]  Migliorini (1960), 246; Wallenstein (1912).
[118]  Chiappelli (1969), 24ff.
[119]  All these examples from the first page of the first volume of Sanudo (1879–1903).

phrases in his vernacular text, probably because equivalents were lacking in his native Polish (we cannot be sure of the explanation until the contexts in which Latin phrases were used have received more careful and systematic study).[120]

The final question to be addressed in this essay is the one which social historians are likely to consider the most important. Who employed Latin in the ways described above? The conventional response to the question is 'the educated class', in the sense of adult male clerics, nobles and professional men, especially in the sixteenth and seventeenth centuries. According to this conventional view, early modern Europe was divided into two cultures, an international learned culture based on Latin and a popular culture based on the local vernaculars. For a dramatic illustration of this binary opposition, we may turn to the city of Metz in January 1502, when the bishop had a comedy of Terence performed in the original Latin, and a riot ensued because the ordinary people in the audience could not understand what was going on.[121]

All the same, this conventional wisdom is inadequate. In the first place, it is not too difficult to find examples of people without the Latin conventionally expected of them. Priests, for example, as the bishops of the counter-reformation discovered when they visited their dioceses. Rulers did not always know Latin, thus creating complications for foreign diplomats. The Burgundian chronicler Georges Chastellain tells a story about Philip the Good failing to understand a speech made to him in Latin.[122] That some Renaissance noblemen were in the same situation is suggested by treatises such as the *Ricordi* (1554) by Saba da Castiglione, knight of Malta, written expressly for young *cavalieri* without a knowledge of Latin. Some scholars appear to have found it difficult to speak Latin. Holberg's comments on eighteenth-century Oxford have already been discussed. Even in Renaissance Italy, some famous scholars appear to have had little facility in speaking Latin. When the Emperor Frederick III visited Florence in 1453, the humanist Carlo Marsuppini was unable to

---

[120] Pasek (1929). On the first page alone there are six Latin phrases, *ex commiseratione, ab antiquo, innatum odium, in vicinitate, oppressit, per amorem gentis nostrae*. On this practice, Backvis (1958).
[121] Vigneulles (1927–33), vol. 4, 15.
[122] Chastellain (1863), 66.

make the Latin oration expected of him, while a scholar of the calibre of Carlo Sigonio appears to have failed to communicate in Latin with a French visitor.[123]

The people who lacked the knowledge they should have possessed are perhaps less interesting and less surprising than the examples of people who possessed the knowledge they should (according to the conventional wisdom) have lacked. If the accounts of Oxford and Cambridge colleges were kept in Latin, this suggests that the clerks as well as the fellows understood that language.

Again, European women seem to have known more Latin than they have generally been given credit for. Queen Elizabeth's skill in Latin has already been made obvious enough, and she was far from the only Renaissance lady to handle that language with competence. The Renaissance Princess Isabella d'Este spoke Latin. Other ladies, such as Isotta Nogarola, wrote it with an ease and elegance which entitles them to be called 'humanists'.[124] As late as the eighteenth century, a princess without scholarly pretensions, Sophia, mother of George I, spoke Latin.[125]

Even women of low status might understand something of the language. The famous Estienne family of printers spoke Latin at table in their house in Paris 'so that the very maidservants came to understand what was said and even to speak it a little'.[126] The situation in the Montaigne household must have been a similar one if the young Michel was able to grow up speaking Latin as his first language. A still more unusual case was that of the blind girl George Borrow met at Manzanares, who told him in Latin that she had been taught the language by a Jesuit.[127]

Still more surprising are cases of lower-class males who knew Latin without these upper-class contacts. A sixteenth-century Venetian shoemaker, for example, explaining his theological views to the Inquisition, switched to Latin to say that 'God wants everyone to be saved' ('Deus vult omnes homines salvos fieri').[128] Of course this case may have been exceptional. But we should remember the evidence of travellers that in East-Central Europe at least,

---

[123]    On Marsuppini, Vespasiano (1970–6), vol. 1, 519; on Sigonio, De Thou (1838), 280.
[124]    Grafton and Jardine (1986), ch. 2.
[125]    Walpole (1924), 121.
[126]    Quoted in Armstrong (1954), 15–16.
[127]    Borrow (1843), 216.
[128]    Mackenney (1987), 184.

some innkeepers and coachmen spoke Latin, or at least enough of it to communicate with Englishmen and Frenchmen. There is a geography of Latin as well as a sociology.

This is the place to record a few examples of non-Europeans who knew Latin, from the anonymous Turk who spoke Latin to Coryate in France to Rustam Khan, who spoke Latin to François Bernier in India.[129] On his mission to Ethiopia in 1520, Francisco Alvares was interrogated by King Lebna Dengel through a Latin interpreter. On a similar mission to Shah Abbas of Persia, in 1620, the imperial ambassador delivered a speech in Latin which was translated by someone at court.[130] At least one Asian ruler of the period knew Latin himself: Prince Karaéng Pattingalloang of Macassar.[131]

There is also a chronology of Latin, and here too the conventional wisdom needs correction. Latin did not suddenly disappear at the end of the seventeenth or even the end of the eighteenth century. It was still being spoken and written in some places and in some domains in the nineteenth century and even the twentieth. Its empire may have contracted in the later seventeenth century, and if this turns out to be the case, it would give the universal language schemes of the period an added significance, an added urgency.[132] Ironically enough, however, John Wilkins's treatise *Towards a Real Character and a Philosophical Language* was itself one of the works of the period which was translated into Latin.

In any case, these universal language schemes bore little practical fruit until the late nineteenth century. Ludovic Zamenhof, for example, published the first book in Esperanto, *Internacia Linguo*, in 1887. As these two words suggest, Esperanto is virtually a simplified form of Latin, despite or because of the fact that it was devised in eastern Europe.

The conventional view of the history of Latin is that it declined because it was not adapted to the modern world, because it could not change with the times and incorporate new words for new or newly discovered phenomena.[133] I have tried to suggest that, on the contrary, it is the practical uses of Latin, on which I have

[129]  Morison (1927), 88.
[130]  Ijsewijn (1987), 101.
[131]  Lombard (1990), 107–8.
[132]  On these schemes, Knowlson (1975); Slaughter (1982).
[133]  For an example of this type of criticism, Slaughter (1982), 73–4.

placed particular emphasis in this paper, which help explain why its use was so widespread and why it survived so long. It was indeed convenient for students to have some chance of understanding lectures in universities all over Europe, and when Latin declined, so did the custom of the 'academic tour', *peregrinatio academica*, no less important than the better-known Grand Tour. It was also convenient for diplomats, travellers and traders to have a lingua franca.

Of course, these conveniences had their price. For example, the use of Latin made the gap between elite culture and popular culture wider than it might otherwise have been. It also excluded women from much of high culture. The decline of Latin in the eighteenth century is surely associated with the rise of a female reading public at much the same time and in much the same places. The sociolinguists are surely right to stress the cumulative element in 'language shift', the extent to which particular languages spread because they are perceived to spread, (since parents come to think that it would be useful for their children to learn them), and conversely, decline because they are perceived to decline.[134]

It would surely be wrong, however, to explain the rise and fall of Latin in purely practical terms. 'Latin to survive' was important, as Bassompierre's memoirs brought home to us, but there was also 'Latin to impress', a sign of distinction. Its importance in this respect is revealed, for example, in the language of quackery, especially in the advertisements for remedies such as the *Elixir Vitae, Aqua Celestis,* or *Pillulae Radiis Solis Extractae.*[135] One late seventeenth-century quack bill even advertised the fact that its hero, among other skills, 'speaks Latin' to 'strangers that cannot speak English'.[136] It is stretching the meaning of a technical term too far to describe the study of Latin as a 'Renaissance puberty rite', but the suggestion that it was studied in part because it both conferred and symbolized status has much to be said for it.[137]

An attraction for some, to others Latin was like a red rag to a bull. To the Quakers and others it was 'the language of the

---

[134]   Wall (1969).
[135]   Porter (1987), 89.
[136]   The address 'At the Sign of the Moon and Stars in Leopard's Court in Baldwins Garden near Holborn'.
[137]   Ong (1959).

Beast', a clear reference to the Church of Rome and a possible reference to the monopolies of the learned which Latin helped defend.[138] To educational reformers such as Christian Thomasius, Latin symbolized scholastic philosophy, or more generally 'the weight of past habits of thought'.[139] Latin was loved and hated not only for what it facilitated or made more difficult, but also for its associations, for what it symbolized.

---

[138] Jones (1953), 314.
[139] Blackall (1959), 13.

# 3

## Language and Identity in Early Modern Italy

'Language is one of the strongest links to the fatherland' ('La lingua è uno dei più forti vincoli che stringe alla patria') (Count Galeani Napione)

The problem of identity is a topical, indeed an all too topical subject, associated as it is with the so-called 'ethnic revival' which extends from the Catalans to the Kurds, from Paisley to Khomeini, from Kenya to Bosnia. The immediacy of the problem has helped to generate some extremely interesting sociological and anthropological studies, which raise questions and employ concepts which may well be useful to historians in their presumptuous enterprise of reconstructing past identities. The labels imposed by outsiders are relatively easy to study; but the inner sense of belonging is much more elusive, and the relation between the two is if anything even more difficult to pin down.

National identity is clearly an important field of study, and it has received a good deal of attention recently, from sociologists and social historians alike.[1] However, even in the modern world of nations it is obvious enough that other types of cultural identity remain significant. In late medieval and early modern Europe the

---

Epigraph from Napione in 1791, quoted in Puppo (1957), 493.

[1] Armstrong (1982); Breuilly (1982); Anderson (1983); Gellner (1983); Hobsbawm (1990); Smith (1986).

rivals to national identity were even more important; regional identities, ethnic identities, civic identities, and religious identities, to say nothing of gender, of family, or of clerical or noble identities (whether or not these should be described in terms of 'class').

This multiplicity, when it is recognized, is sometimes perceived as a 'postmodern' phenomenon. However, to a historian like myself there seems to be nothing uniquely postmodern, or even modern, about it. I would even be prepared to suggest that postmodernity comes easily to some peoples, such as the Italians, precisely because they have such strong premodern traditions, having invested relatively little of their energies in what has become an old-fashioned 'modern' national identity.

What exactly makes for a strong sense of identity? Is it always, or at least generally, 'reactive', that is, a reaction to contact with other cultures and the threat of losing ourselves in them?[2] Does it necessarily develop, as two historians of the modern Swedish middle class has put it, 'in both dependence on and opposition to other social units'?[3]

A historian of early modern Europe can testify that in that culture (or cluster of cultures), at least, the identity of a community was often defined by opposition, taking the form of the rejection of the customs of the 'other', as in the case of the Huguenots in France, whose identity rested to a significant degree on their rejection of Catholicism.[4] A similar point might be made about English popular Protestantism, with its slogan 'No Popery', from the late sixteenth to the early nineteenth century, as it may be about northern Irish Protestantism to this day. In a similar manner, in Japan, a country with relatively little direct experience of foreigners between the mid-seventeenth and mid-nineteenth centuries, the visits of the Korean embassies made a great impression and were re-enacted in popular festivals, because they helped in the construction of a Japanese identity.[5]

In cases like these, boundaries are crucial – cultural boundaries, in other words symbolic boundaries. Identities generally depend on stereotypes of the self and also stereotypes of others, like the

---

[2] Cohen (1982); cf. Carneiro da Cunha (1986).
[3] Frykman and Löfgren (1987).
[4] Joutard (1977), 40.
[5] Toby (1986).

Protestant stereotype of the Catholic or 'Papist', or the Christian stereotypes of the Muslim and the Jew. Identities rely on what Freud once called, in a famous phrase, 'the narcissism of small differences', exaggerating whatever makes one community distinct from others.[6] Definitions of identity frequently involve attempts to present culture as if it were nature, as in the case of the widespread myth of special blood: English blood, blue blood, 'pure' Catholic blood (limpieza de sangre), etc.

To a historian, however, it is obvious that (given the ways in which they have changed over time) cultural identities must be artifacts or even inventions.[7] 'Invention' may be too dramatic a term, implying a self-consciousness which often seems to have been lacking in practice, but the process of identity formation has to be viewed as a collective construction. A distinguished literary historian of Renaissance England has written a study of what he calls the 'self-fashioning' of leading writers such as Sir Thomas More and Sir Thomas Wyatt, and of the heroes of Marlowe and Shakespeare.[8] Collective identities may be analysed – and are being analysed – in a similar way. The conclusion of a recent anthropological study of Morocco, for example, is that spite of attempts to make them hard and sharp, identities often seem to be fluid, fragile or 'negotiable'.[9] They are also context-specific in the sense that the same people present themselves differently in different situations.

The relative importance of each of these multiple identities for particular individuals and groups, their priorities, in other words the hierarchy of identities, is a question which historians ought to take seriously, however difficult it may be to answer. Another problem which they surely need to consider is whether these identities were expressed or whether they were constructed by media such as language or ritual. Cultural historians used to assume that the outward forms of culture 'expressed' or 'reflected' some deeper inward reality. Nowadays this assumption is often criticized as too reductionist or determinist and the metaphor currently favoured is not 'reflection' but 'construction'. The reaction was salutary but it may have gone too far, in the sense of

[6]  Freud (1930), 90.
[7]  Hobsbawm and Ranger (1983).
[8]  Greenblatt (1980).
[9]  Rosen (1984), ch. 2.

encouraging us to forget the constraints on collective creativity. The historical record does not suggest that collective identities can be invented or constructed at will. Some attempts at construction are successful, others fail, and it is for historians to discover why this should have been the case.

Identities are also 'embodied' – to employ a more neutral metaphor – in such media as ritual, myth and material culture. In the case of myth, obvious examples are narratives about the origin of a particular community, like the stories of Trojan descent so common in the sixteenth century in Britain, France and elsewhere (the city of Padua, for example, claimed to have been founded by the Trojan Antenor).[10] Rituals too can help define the identity of a group not only by excluding non-members from participation but also by symbolic attacks on the enemies of the community. In some parts of Europe, formerly frontiers between Christianity and Islam, from Spain to Croatia, ritual battles between 'Moors' and 'Christians' are still re-enacted every year. In Britain, the celebration of Guy Fawkes' Day on 5 November took, and in some places still takes the form of burning the pope, a ritual expressing traditional Protestant values.

As for material culture, the Catholic abstinence from meat, especially in Protestant countries, and the Dutch concern – or even, as foreigners might say, the Dutch obsession – with cleanliness have each been interpreted by recent historians as affirmations of difference from others, in other words as badges of identity.[11] A similar point might be made and indeed has been made by Pierre Bourdieu about conspicuous consumption as a means of distinguishing oneself from others.[12]

Another factor which must not be omitted in the study of collective identity is what might be called 'social memory', the image of a group's past shared by members of that group.[13] Who we are depends on who we were. However, there is a significant circularity involved here: who we think we were depends on who we think we are.

For this reason, historians have often played an important role in the affirmation of national and other solidarities.

[10]  Giovanni da Nono (1934–9).
[11]  Douglas (1966); Bossy (1975), 109; Schama (1987), 375ff.
[12]  Bourdieu (1979).
[13]  Nora (1984–6), vol.1; Burke (1989); Fentress and Wickham (1992).

'Possession of a history that is not shared gives the group its identity.'[14] In the creation of the Dutch nation in the sixteenth and seventeenth centuries, for example, the myth of the ancient Batavians and their resistance to Rome was of considerable importance, and it is interesting to find that the Dutch attributed the virtue of cleanliness to their Batavian ancestors.[15]

One of the most important of the signs of collective identity is language. Speaking the same language, or variety of language, as someone else is a simple and effective way of indicating solidarity; speaking a different language or variety of language is an equally effective way of distinguishing oneself from other individuals or groups. A number of sociolinguistic studies have examined language from this point of view.[16]

For J. G. Herder, in his essay *Uber den Ursprung der Sprache* (1772) and also for the romantics, language was of course the sign of identity *par excellence*. A recent historical essay on romantic nationalism suggests with some plausibility that it was no accident that this movement arose at about the same time as the new philosophy of language associated with Humboldt, Grimm and others, which stressed the way in which languages influence their users.[17] Sociolinguistic research has confirmed the importance of links between language and group consciousness. For example, in a famous study of an island off the coast of Massachusetts, Martha's Vineyard, William Labov investigated what he called 'the social motivation of a sound change', demonstrating that the people who were more attached to the local community were also the ones to keep up the traditional pronunciation.[18]

However, the romantic assumption of a necessary link between language and national consciousness been challenged by sociolinguists on one side and students of nationalism on the other. For example, one recent study of ethnic communities declared firmly that language 'is not decisive for constituting identity', while another launched an attack on scholars who 'persist in regarding language as the distinguishing mark of ethnicity', and

---

[14]  Zonabend (1980), 203. Cf. Pina Cabral (1987).
[15]  Schama (1987), 78.
[16]  Gumperz (1982b); Edwards (1985); Le Page and Tabouret-Keller (1985).
[17]  Nipperdey (1983).
[18]  Labov (1972a), 1–42.

in ignoring the fact that the sense of community among the Scots, for example, or among the Welsh has little to do with the ability to speak Gaelic.[19] A similar point has been made about the Basques today. 'One is Basque by descent; if one can speak Basque that is a good thing, but if one does not speak it, there are still plenty of reasons to be Basque rather than something else.'[20] Again, a recent anthropological study of the Bretons has emphasized the 'mis-match' between language and patriotism there.[21]

From the other side, a leading sociologist of language has questioned the generalization that 'language maintenance is a function of group membership or group loyalty'.[22] My purpose here, however, is to explore the place of language among other signs of identity (or props to identity), not to argue which of them is the most important. The association between language and identity which the romantics believed to be universal seems, like so many so-called universals of human nature, to be subject to change over time.

The remainder of this essay is concerned with Italy from 1500 to 1800, or more exactly, if we are looking for more natural limits (as Marc Bloch recommended historians to do), with Italy from the time of Dante, when the *questione della lingua* became a matter of lively controversy, to the Risorgimento, when some of the leaders of the movement for a united Italy argued, like Massimo d'Azeglio, that language 'constitutes nationhood' ('costituisce la nazionalità'). There were, however, more than ten million Italians alive at any one moment in this long period, and we know little about the attitudes of most of them. The reader should bear in mind that the evidence is patchy, limited almost entirely to a minority of adult males living in towns.

To begin with the most obvious, the most frequently discussed and the most controversial question of all. To what extent did the people of this period consider themselves as 'Italian'? As early as the fourteenth century, a few writers identified themselves as Italian in certain contexts. The merchant-chronicler Giovanni Villani expressed a sense of Italian superiority to the north. So

[19]  Armstrong (1982), 241ff.; Smith (1986), 27.
[20]  Wardhaugh (1987), 125.
[21]  McDonald (1989).
[22]  Fishman (1972), 96.

did the humanist Coluccio Salutati, who was contemptuous of 'French levity' ('Gallicam levitatem') and concerned with the *libertas Italiae*. Salutati once described himself, with fascinating precision, as 'Italian by race, Florentine by fatherland' ('gente Italicus, patria Florentinus').[23] In a famous poem, Petrarch wrote of the traditional valour of the *Italici* and also of 'my Italy', *Italia mia*.

Expressions of this kind become more frequent from the sixteenth century onwards. This dating suggests that the French invasion of 1494 created or at least encouraged some kind of solidarity against the foreigners, the 'barbarians', thus illustrating the point made by the sociologists about the importance of 'reactive' identity. The king of France, Charles VIII, was accused of aiming at 'the dominion of the whole of Italy' ('il dominio di tutta Italia'), and there were soon attempts to form an 'Italian league' against him (*unione di Italia*). The poet Boiardo lamented the sight of Italy in flames ('la Italia tutta a fiamma e a foco'). Machiavelli's *Prince* quoted Petrarch's poem about the valour of the *Italici* and exhorted rulers to drive out the 'barbarous' foreigners at much the same time as Pope Julius II uttered his famous cry, 'out with the barbarians' ('fuori i barbari').

Phrases like *Itala gens* or *la stirpe italiana*, in other words the Italian 'race' or 'family', became more frequent and perhaps acquired a greater resonance than in the days of Salutati.[24] At the end of the sixteenth century, a Genoese patrician, Andrea Spinola, could refer to himself as 'a good Italian', *buon italiano*.[25] A different kind of evidence suggesting that Italian identity was indeed being taken more seriously than before is the existence of Guicciardini's *Storia d'Italia*, written in the 1540s and published in the 1550s, a history which broke with the tradition of writing separate accounts of the different city-states and kingdoms and presented Italian history from 1494 onwards as a whole. Another piece of evidence which points in this direction is Girolamo Muzio's plea for the union of Italy, published in 1572.[26]

In short, in the writings of intellectuals after 1494 there are far more signs of consciousness of being Italian than there were

[23]   De Rosa (1980), 87–99.
[24]   Gilbert (1954); Ilardi (1956); Marcu (1976), 29ff.; Denis (1979), 109ff.
[25]   Spinola (1981), 247.
[26]   Muzio (1572).

before that date. To interpret this change, however, is more difficult than it may look. This pan-Italian consciousness should not be equated with modern nationalism (as it was by nineteenth-century Italians in search of a genealogy).[27] It tended to take the traditional form of xenophobia and generally lacked the distinctively nationalist demand that a 'people' should be organized in one political unit. A similar point might be made about the early eighteenth-century writers who began to use the term *nazione* in a new sense, 'no longer ethnic but cultural'.[28]

Of course, Italy was – and to some extent still is – the classic ground of *campanilismo*. In the early modern period, despite the decline of the autonomous city-state, local (especially civic) identity remained important. People seem to have thought of themselves as Florentines, Venetians, Genoese and so on rather than Italians. As we have seen, the humanist Salutati used the emotionally laden word *patria* to describe his loyalty to Florence, not to Italy. For Machiavelli, 'our nation' (*nazione nostra*) was Florence, Italy merely a *provincia*.[29]

In a similar way, later in the sixteenth century, a Florentine tailor, Sebastiano Arditi, uses the term *Italia* from time to time in his journal but expresses an emotion about a place only when he writes about 'The honour of my poor fatherland, the city of Florence' ('l'onore della povera patria mia, città di Fiorenza').[30] The parish, the ward (*contrada*) or the neighbourhood (*vicinanza*) also seem to have been a focus of loyalty in some cities, as in the case of Florence, which has been studied with particular care and intensity in recent years.[31]

These multiple local identities were expressed – or perhaps created – by civic rituals, images and myths. The myths included stories of the origin of cities. The Venetians, for example, associated their liberty with their foundation by refugees from the barbarian invasions. As for the Florentines, in the time of Dante they believed that their city had been founded by Caesar. In the age of Salutati and Bruni, on the other hand, c.1400, they argued that it had been founded during the Roman republic, a shift

[27] For example Pasquale Villari, discussed by Gilbert (1954), 38ff.
[28] Folena (1983), 22.
[29] Chabod (1961), 173ff.
[30] Arditi (1970), 29, 107, 129 (Italia), 50 (Firenze).
[31] Kent (1978); Kent and Kent (1982). On multiple identity in Renaissance Italy, Weissman (1985).

which expresses the increased emphasis on republican liberty in the age of the Florentine struggle for survival, in other words the attempt to avoid being swallowed by Milan: a struggle which made them more conscious of what they stood for, of who they were.[32] Reactive identity again.

The importance of the process of 'identification' with ancient Rome in the Renaissance will be obvious enough. Individuals like the humanist Pomponio Leto in Rome or the painter Andrea Mantegna in Mantua and their respective circles playfully adopted Roman names and titles.[33] Milanese, Florentines and Venetians alike claimed to be 'new Romans'. There were biblical as well as classical props to identity; the Florentines, for example, saw themselves as the chosen people and their city as the New Jerusalem.[34]

Imagery reinforced this identification, presenting Florence in the form of Jerusalem in some manuscripts, or presenting the struggle of Florence with Milan in Donatello's sculptures in the shape of David's combat with Goliath or St George's with the dragon. Civic rituals also made their contribution to civic identity, with the feast of the patron saint of the city (St John the Baptist in Florence, St Mark in Venice) as an obvious example.

In Venice, in particular, there was a whole series of urban rituals which communicated and created a sense of what it was to be Venetian. Some celebrated the city as a whole, some appealed to the loyalty of particular quarters, as in the case of the famous 'fist war' (guerra de'pugni) fought in the sixteenth, seventeenth and eighteenth centuries between the Castellani and the Nicolotti, battles for bridges which symbolized the liminal space between two urban territories. There was a similar battle for a bridge in Pisa between the northerners and the southerners, still fought in the early nineteenth century, a survival from a large number of similar ritualized contests of the late Middle Ages between quarters of a particular city. In a similar way, even today, the Sienese Palio still expresses and reinforces the rivalry between the different contrade of the city.[35]

---

[32]   Baron (1955).
[33]   On Leto, Wardrop (1963), 20–3; on Mantegna, Saxl (1957).
[34]   On Venice as new Rome, Chambers (1970), ch. 1; Tafuri (1984). On Florence as new Jerusalem, Chastel (1954); Weinstein (1968).
[35]   Details in Burke (c.1993b).

These civic identities coexisted with other corporate identities, which persisted despite the claim of the nineteenth-century historian Jacob Burckhardt that they disappeared in what he called the age of 'the development of the individual'.[36] Italian cities continued to be full of *compagnie*, voluntary associations which created their own loyalties. The religious fraternities are probably the best known of these associations.[37] Their members sometimes came from one ethnic group, as in the cases of the fraternities of the Greeks and the Slavs in Venice, which would seem to have been both expressing and defending an identity threatened by submersion in the melting-pot of the big city.

Nor should we forget the existence of other kinds of voluntary association such as the many more or less learned academies, with their distinctive names and devices, and other kinds of club like the *compagnie delle calze* in Venice, which wore special costumes as well as organizing amateur dramatics. Guild identities were also strong in Italian cities, while a recent historian has analysed journeymen's rituals in sixteenth century Venice as 'an effort to forge a sense of community'.[38]

Then we come to social class. The best-known model of society in early modern Europe was that of the three estates, those who pray, those who fight and those who work.[39] However, urban Italians preferred another ternary model, a good deal closer to that of class. It consisted of the rich, or more exactly the 'fat', the *popolo grasso*; the 'little people', or *popolo minuto*; and those in the middle, the *mediocri*.[40]

The importance of this form of social consciousness relative to other forms of collective identity is not easy to assess. Patricians had a strong sense of being patricians, guildsmen some sense of being guildsmen (as well as members of a particular guild), and so on. The difficulty lies in discovering the extent to which these horizontal solidarities cut across regional or city boundaries. That patricians and nobles had some sense of belonging to a common group is suggested by the fact that they not infrequently married into families from other cities; as Lorenzo de' Medici, to

---

[36]   Burckhardt (1860), ch. 2.
[37]   Weissmann (1982).
[38]   Martin (1987), 208. Cf. Cerutti (1988, 1992) on eighteenth-century Turin.
[39]   Niccoli (1979).
[40]   Gilbert (1965), 23–8.

quote a famous example, married into the Roman baronial family of the Orsini. There was thus some 'transregional feeling' already in existence, which the French invasion was able to activate and strengthen.[41]

Whether this kind of group consciousness was expressed by particular forms of language it is difficult to say. Perhaps only an Englishman would think of asking such a question, since England was and is a country where varieties of language are associated rather closely with social classes. However, it is surely significant to find some sixteenth-century Italians claiming to be able to recognize Tuscan peasants by their archaic speech, and explaining these archaisms by the fact that 'the peasants speak less to out-siders than townspeople do, and so change less' ('i contadini conversano manco con forestieri che non fanno i cittadini, e però mutano manco').[42] A Neapolitan nobleman of the same period, the Marchese Del Tufo, expressed his contempt for the 'coarse speech of the people' ('il parlar goffo della plebe'), while a few years later, the town clerk of Naples, G. C. Capaccio, contrasted 'the Neapolitan in the mouth of the nobles' ('il parlare napoletano nelle bocche dei Nobili') with that of the *plebe*.[43]

In discussing this wide range of potential or actual identities I do not mean to give the impression that Italians of the early modern period were to be envied in this respect. It is at least equally possible that they had too many roles to play for comfort, and more than one historian has described them as suffering from 'identity crisis', though it is not easy to see what evidence for such a crisis there might be.[44]

At this point it should at last be possible to engage with the problem of the relation between language and identity in early modern Italy. Curiously enough, the problem has not been studied intensively, despite the fact that Italian linguists take history very seriously indeed. The best-known history of the Italian language has little to say about society. Although a fine social history of Italian exists, it starts only in 1860.[45]

So far as the early modern period is concerned, one might

[41]  Ilardi (1956), 344.
[42]  On the peasants, Castiglione (1528), 1.31; Borghini (1971), 139. Cf. Brunet (1976), esp. 220ff.
[43]  Tagliareni (1954); Capaccio (1882), 538.
[44]  Becker (1971); Ascoli (1987), 43.
[45]  Migliorini (1960); De Mauro (1976).

reasonably start from the fact that certain ethnic groups in Italy affirmed their separate cultural identity by speaking languages other than Italian. There were speakers of German and 'Slav' (*Schiavo*, in other words Croat) in the north, and German speakers of a sort of 'pidgin-Italian' wherever the notorious German mercenaries or *Lanzknechts* were to be found.[46] There were speakers of Greek in the south and also in Venice, where it is possible to find evidence of a man dictating his will in that language, and of wise women such as a certain Serena or 'Marietta Greca' impressing their clients by praying over them in Greek.[47] There were speakers of Hebrew and Ladino among the Jewish communities everywhere.

In the thirteenth century, French, especially in the form now called *franco-veneto*, was regularly spoken and written in northern Italy, as the history of Venice by Martin da Canal (*Les estoires de Venise*) and the travels of Marco Polo (originally known as the *Divisament dou monde*) should remind us, while later in the Middle Ages this spoken language seems to have been associated with what sociolinguists would call the 'speech domain' of chivalry, from the performances on the piazza of itinerant singers of tales to the mottos accompanying the *imprese* or devices used in tournaments (as in the case of the Medici motto, *Le temps revient*).[48] In the late fifteenth century, when the Catalans Calixtus III and Alexander VI were popes, Catalan was spoken at the court of Rome, even by Castilians.[49] Again, in Italy as else-where in Europe, the use of Latin by the learned might be analysed not only as a language of convenience, a lingua franca, but also as an affirmation of the separate cultural identity of scholars (above, p. 40).

However, this essay will concentrate on different forms of Italian. An obvious case of the association between language and identity is that of the secret language or 'jargon' (*gergo, lingua zerga, furbesco*) of beggars and thieves, recorded in some detail from the fifteenth century onwards but doubtless much older. According to the *Nuovo modo di intendere la lingua zerga* (1545), for example, thieves were 'fishermen' (*pescatori*) or 'carps'

[46] Coates (1969).
[47] Burke (1987), 213–14.
[48] Paccagnella (1984, 1987). Cf. Folena (1964).
[49] Batllori (1983).

(*carpioni*), while to speak was 'to sing' (canzonare), and the jargon itself was known as 'counterpoint' (*contrapunto*).[50]

A secret language had its practical convenience for a group on the margin of respectable society, but the jargon was also a means of identification of the group in the eyes (or rather the ears) of outsiders. We may also suspect that it was a badge of identity for group members.

Less exotic but much more important is regional dialect, because it was the first and probably the only language of the majority of the population. As late as 1860, when Italy was officially united, it is probable that only 3 per cent of the population understood Italian, let alone spoke it.[51] Regional dialect identified the speakers most clearly to outsiders. The best evidence of the practice of labelling people by their dialect comes from comedy, more especially the sixteenth-century *commedia dell'arte*, in which a number of ridiculous figures with regional accents make their appearance, notably the servant or porter from Bergamo. Like the inhabitants of other highland zones, the people of the Bergamo are a frequently migrated in search of work in early modern Italy, and their main goal seems to have been Venice, a cosmopolitan city where the evidence of plays suggests that the inhabitants were unusually language conscious.

To decode the comedies of Andrea Calmo, such as *La Spagnolas*, for example, played in Venice in the mid-sixteenth century, it is necessary to be familiar with four or five versions of colloquial Italian, not only that of the Bergamask servant but that of the Venetian merchant, the Bolognese pedant, the Greek-Italian of the Balkan mercenary soldier or *stradiotto*, and so on. This 'literary multilingualism' has generally been analysed as an example of literary playfulness and self-consciousness.[52] It should also, perhaps, be interpreted as a humorous-hostile reaction of Venetians to the invasion of their city by immigrants.

Whether dialect was generally a badge of identity for insiders is more doubtful, because ordinary people were not expected to speak anything else. Here too, however, we need to think about reactive identities. It is so common for groups to think that their way of life is the only way of life for human beings that definite

50  Camporesi (1973). Cf. Aquilecchia (1967).
51  De Mauro (1976).
52  Paccagnella (1984); Stussi (1972), 703ff. Cf. Lazzerini (1978), esp. 125ff.

cultural identities seem to develop only when diverse groups come into contact, and above all when one group tries to make another conform to its model. Just as the consciousness of identity is forged in situations of contact and conflict, so the signs or badges of identity become signs only when someone else is trying to eliminate them. Could pride in *bergamasco* on the part of insiders well be a reaction to mocking ethnic labelling by outsiders?

It is hard to do more than speculate about the way in which the peasants viewed or constructed their identity. The written sources of peasant speech which have survived were produced by outsiders, notably playwrights such as Ruzante, Giovanmaria Cecchi and Alessandro Piccolomini, or the clerks to courts in which country people were interrogated.[53] For this reason it is advisable to limit this discussion to better-documented groups, especially the upper classes.

It is fairly clear that Italian nobles or patricians employed their local dialects throughout the early modern period. The difficulty is to discover what this linguistic practice meant to them. The most prudent way to investigate the problem might be to try to describe before attempting to interpret, in other words to attempt to establish the implicit rules which governed switches between dialect and the forms of standardized Italian which will be discussed later.

Members of the upper classes did not only speak dialect to people who could speak nothing else, like their servants. They also spoke it to one another on certain occasions, some of them festive, others more serious or formal. Dialect was regularly employed by the upper classes on festive occasions, perhaps as a conscious marker of such occasions. For example, a festive society of noblemen and others (including the painter G. P. Lomazzo), the Academigli dor Compa Zavargna, which existed in Milan at the beginning of the seventeenth century, deliberately spoke the dialect of the Valle di Bregno. This valley happened to be the area of origin of the wine porters of the city of Milan, so that the dialect became associated with wine and more generally with festivity.[54]

What did this practice mean? It is conceivable that patricians were identifying themselves with ordinary people and thinking

[53] Brunet (1976).
[54] Lomazzo (1627). Cf. Lynch (1966).

that we are all equal while we laugh, but this suggestion (developed in a famous study by Mikhail Bakhtin) may well be anachronistic.[55] We have already seen some evidence of contempt on the part of nobles for what one of them, in sixteenth-century Naples, called the *parlar goffo della plebe*. An alternative interpretation of this use of dialect would be that the upper classes associated the low and the comic in an Aristotelian way, or more exactly a neo-Aristotelian way, in conformity with the humanist interpretations of the *Poetics*.

In Venice at least, dialect was employed in some formal situations. For example, patricians spoke Venetian at meetings of the Great Council and the Senate, while advocates spoke it in the courts.[56] In these cases the use of dialect would seem to mark or symbolize Venetian autonomy and Venetian identity.

Venetian dialect was also written on occasions. A famous example from the early sixteenth century is the diary kept by the patrician Marin Sanudo, which has been printed and runs to fifty-eight volumes. Sanudo may be expressing Venetian patriotism by his choice of code but he may simply be old-fashioned in his resistance to the Tuscanization promoted, ironically enough, by a colleague of his, another Venetian patrician, Pietro Bembo. The choice of Venetian by the painter Marco Boschini in his *Carta de navegar pittoresco* (1660) is a self-conscious expression at once of local patriotism and of a sense of the decorum of his speech domain. As he put it himself, 'Do I, who am a Venetian in Venice, and speak of Venetian painters, have to wear clothes which are not my own?' ('Mi, che son venezian in Venezia, e che parlo de pitori veneziani, ho da andarme a stravestir?').[57]

In the case of the love poems of Maffeo Venier, such as the famous *La Strazzosa*, Venetian dialect (like Roman dialect in the work of Pietro Aretino) marks out the poet's position in a linguistic-literary debate. His description of an interior with a cat, an old servant, hens, children, etc., expresses his opposition to the artificial conventions of Petrarchism, if not in the name of realism, then at least in the name of the domestic, *alla demèstega*, or the grotesque ('Onde se vede un ordene a grottesche / De persone, de bestie et de baltresche').[58]

---

[55] Bakhtin (1965).
[56] Vianello (1957).
[57] Quoted by Cortelazzo (1983), 367.
[58] Dazzi (1956), vol. 1, 395–99.

In the case of some Venetian political poetry of the seventeenth century written in dialect, however, the explanation for the choice is probably more complex. Some of the poems are written in the name of ordinary people and criticize the government. Take, for example, the *Lamento dei pescatori veneziani* (which has been dated to *c.*1570). The poem expresses the solidarity of those who were born between the canals, whether they are rich or poor.

> peché non avémo sodi o possession
> semo pur nassù tutti in t'i canài.

Excluded from this solidarity – in a typical expression of the ethnocentrism of 'poor whites' – are the foreign immigrants and other despicable people, such as thieves, peasants, whores and cuckolds:

> Nessun d'e' notti fu giego o schiaón,
> Zudio, furatolé, mulo o vilan,
> Né puttana, né becco, né monton.

The anonymous author of this poem, despite his use of 'we', is more likely than not to have been upper class.[59] If so, his use of dialect may be interpreted in several different ways. It may act as a marker of a particular genre. It may express an identification with ordinary people. However, we should also take into account the possibility that the author is using the argument that the people are against the policies of the government as a weapon in a contest between noble factions.

A similar set of problems is raised by an early seventeenth-century dialect poem called the *Piffania di Pizzocan,* in which the speakers, the inhabitants of Burano, beg the Pope not to lift the interdict he had placed on the city in 1606, on the grounds that they had never been better off for bread and wine, and that the interdict must be the reason for this prosperity. Since it was the patriciate, or a group within the patriciate, who resisted the Pope's demands, one might reasonably read the poem as a message to Rome about the popular support for their policies.[60]

Another interesting case, less studied than the Venetian, of the

[59]   Dazzi (1956), vol. 1, 444ff.
[60]   Venice, Biblioteca Marziana, ms Ital. 1818 (= 9436), book 3.

use of dialect in written communication by nobles is the case of
Genoa, and in particular that of a collection of poems printed in
1595, the *Rime Zeneixe*. To put this text back into its sociocultural
context is really a task for specialists, but an outsider like myself
may perhaps be allowed to offer a few speculative remarks.

The dedication of the collection to a certain B. C., 'patrician of
Genoa', refers to 'some verses he composed for his amusement',
suggesting – as in the case of the Valle di Bregno – the association, for patricians, between dialect and relaxation. Indeed, there
was also an association with drink, in the case of a poem
addressed to the humanist Paolo Foglietta in the name of 'Buxoto
innkeeper of Reco'.[61] Playfulness seems uppermost in the translation of the first canto of the *Orlando Furioso* into Genoese, as
well as in a collection of riddles (*demande d'adavina*).

However, other items in the anthology suggest alternative
meanings for the use of dialect. A series of sonnets on the toga
lament the changes in the costume of the patricians and recall
with nostalgia the days of 'That old Roman republic which knew
how to rule the world' ('Quell'antiga Repubrica Romanna / Chi
ha sapuo ro mondo comandà'). Here the use of dialect would seem
to support a call for a return to Genoese republican traditions.

These examples are perhaps already ambiguous or ambivalent
enough. However, it is necessary to complicate the problem even
further by introducing the factor of change over the long term. In
Italy, as in other parts of Europe, the attitude of the upper classes
to regional dialects changed in the course of the early modern
period. There are three main phases. The first phase is that of the
unselfconscious use of dialect by nobles and scholars as well as
everyone else. The second phase is one of deliberate 'withdrawal'
by the upper classes from varieties of language (and indeed other
forms of culture) which they were coming to associate with the
lower elements in society.[62] The third phase – beyond the limits
of this essay – is one of a rediscovery or reappraisal of dialect in
the late eighteenth or early nineteenth centuries, when peasant
speech, like peasant costumes, came to be valued by the upper
classes as symbols of the people or nation.[63] In Italy, for example,
dialect texts and dictionaries were published in the early nine-

[61]  Orero (1595), 102.
[62]  Burke (1978), 270–80.
[63]  Ibid., ch. 1.

teenth century; F. Cherubini's *Vocabolario Milanese-Italiano* (1814) for instance, or B. Gamba's *Collezione delle migliori opere scritte in dialetto veneziano* (1814).

In other words, the upper classes once spoke dialect naturally. Later on, they knew it but tried not to speak it. Finally they tried to speak dialect, because its symbolic associations had become positive, but by that time many of them had probably forgotten it.

The pattern of change seems fairly clear. Where problems arise is in the dating, which varies from region to region, and of course in the relation of this linguistic shift to political developments. Dialect was associated with the people and the people with the nation. On the other hand, regional dialects divided the nation and so to unite the Italians (like the Germans and even the French) it was necessary to encourage a standard language.[64]

To turn at last to this standard language. Since the time of Dante, whose references to what he called 'our vernacular', *lo nostro volgare*, tell us something important about his sense of identity, educated Italians have been interested in what they call the 'language question', *la questione della lingua*; that is, the best form to use in writing and speaking.[65] The problem, as they saw it, was how to communicate across regions. Pierre Bourdieu would doubtless say that the real problem was how to distinguish oneself from the lower classes; he might well be correct, but all the same this is not what the treatises discuss.

Two main solutions to this problem of communication were proposed in the numerous treatises on the subject (most of them dating from the sixteenth century). The first was what might be called the 'eclectic' solution of taking something from each of the main dialects to produce a kind of Italian Esperanto. This was Dante's suggestion in the treatise on the vernacular he wrote in Latin, *De vulgari eloquentia*. What I call rather impolitely 'Esperanto' (and what a number of Italian linguistis call *koinê*) is what Dante called the *vulgaris illustris*, an ideal form of the vernacular. This eclectic language became known in the sixteenth century as *cortegiano*, presumably because it was most often employed in the domain of the court.[66]

[64] Weber (1976), esp. ch. 6.
[65] Hall (1942); Sozzi (1955); Klein (1957); Vitale (1962); Tavoni (1984); Vasoli (1986).
[66] Cremona (1965), 158; Buck (1978).

The second solution, the more successful in the long run, was to adopt one dialect, Tuscan, for polite speech and writing all over Italy, sterilizing its associations with Tuscan identity (just as Danes, for example, or Africans or Japanese use English today without identifying themselves with Britain or the USA). It is of course difficult to sterilize these associations altogether. It was only very slowly that people came to speak of the 'Italian' rather than the Tuscan language, though a reference to *parlare italiano* can be found in the fifteenth century.[67] It is scarcely surprising to find that many of the non-Tuscan participants in the language debate preferred the ultimately unsuccessful Esperanto solution.

The conventional wisdom is that what has been called 'the linguistic unification of the upper classes' took place in Italy in the sixteenth century.[68] It is unlikely, however, that any simple generalization can do justice to the differences between north and south, between men and women, between Tuscan and *cortegiano*, and between oral and written communication.

Evidence about the spoken language in particular is difficult to come by and it cannot always be trusted when it is found. It is fascinating to find a Welshman who lived in Italy in the middle of the sixteenth century, William Thomas, recording that 'all gentlemen do speak the courtesan. For notwithstanding that between the Florentine and the Venetian is great diversity of speech ... yet by the tongue you shall not lightly discern of what part of the country any gentleman is, because that, being children, they are brought up in the courtesan only.'[69] To use such a testimony with any confidence, one needs to know the breadth of the foreigner's experience of different regions, and the depth of his concern with language. Thomas passes these tests reasonably well. He lived in Italy for more than three years, in Venice, Florence, Rome, Naples and elsewhere, and he was sufficiently interested in the language to publish *The Principal Rules of Italian Grammar* on his return to England. However, one would have liked to have asked him some sociolinguistic questions. How were the boys isolated from their local dialect? If upperclass males learned only 'the courtesan', how could they speak to their own mothers and sisters?

---

[67]  Migliorini (1960), 267.
[68]  Hall (1942), 54.
[69]  Thomas (1549), 11–12.

The evidence is of course much better in the case of written communication. In this linguistic domain scholars have suggested that the first phase of the linguistic unification of the peninsula goes back to the fifteenth century, that it took the form of *cortegiano*, and that it is most noticeable in the documents produced by the chanceries of the different Italian states.[70] However, Tuscan elements gradually infiltrated this *koiné*, and from the late sixteenth century onwards Tuscan itself came to be employed increasingly for written communication by the upper classes outside Tuscany.[71]

By the late seventeenth century, the Venetians were practising diglossia, in the sense that although they habitually spoke Venetian, what they wrote was Tuscan.[72] As for the spoken language, a recent study suggests that outside Tuscany before the middle of the eighteenth century, Tuscan was more or less confined to the stage and the pulpit. It was only after 1750 that spoken Tuscan spread more widely, at least in some regions and among some social groups.[73] The Italian linguist Bruno Migliorini once asked rhetorically about this period, 'To what extent and in what way was Italian spoken outside Tuscany?' and answered his question in two words, 'little' and 'badly'.[74] From a social historian's point of view, however, it is significant that a group of Italians was making regular use of a form of speech other than dialect.

How can we explain this (limited) rise of Tuscan? One possible explanation is political. It has been suggested that 'A language is a dialect with an army, navy and air force.'[75] Translating this quip into more pedestrian but more verifiable terms, we are left with the generalization that some dialects become languages not because of their own merit but for political reasons.

There is a good deal of evidence from some parts of Europe in favour of this suggestion, but not in the case of Italy. The hegemony of Tuscan over other regional dialects, its transformation into 'Italian', cannot be explained in political terms as easily as the hegemony of London English or Paris French. The

---

70 General discussion in Durante (1981), 146ff.; for a case-study, Vitale (1953).
71 Durante (1981), 161ff.
72 Cortelazzo (1983), 367.
73 Richardson (1987).
74 Migliorini (1960), 501.
75 An epigram attributed to R. A. Hall.

rise of Tuscan occurred at a time when the peninsula was still politically fragmented. Grand Duke Cosimo de' Medici tried to make what political capital he could out of the rising prestige of Tuscan, but even he did not imagine the possibility of ruling the areas to which his dialect was spreading.[76]

When political unification finally took place, it was the work of Piedmontese like Count Camillo Cavour, who could barely speak Italian, if at all. It was surely writers such as Dante and not politicians such as Cavour who were responsible for the triumph of Tuscan among the Italian upper classes. In the further spread of Italian in the twentieth century the role of the state was more important (via compulsory schooling and conscription), but the role of the media of communication, especially radio and television, was probably still greater.[77]

This reference to the media suggests a second explanation for the rise of Tuscan – the printing press. Its importance as an agent of social and cultural change, including linguistic change, has received considerable emphasis of late. The argument that identical copies of books promoted linguistic standardization, at least in the domain of writing, is one which needs to be taken extremely seriously.[78] Given its natural tendency towards standardization, the press was doubtless important in consolidating the victory of the successful competitor, whichever that variety of language was.

However, it is considerably less plausible to argue that the press played an important part in the rise of Tuscan in the first place. After all, Venice was a more important centre of printing than Florence.

So why did Tuscan triumph? From the point of view of this essay, this is perhaps the wrong question. A discussion of the relation between language and cultural identity ought to concentrate on the rise of transregional languages, rather than on one of them in particular. The rise of both *cortegiano* and Tuscan expressed and encouraged the rise of a transregional consciousness (among upper-class males, at least) between the sixteenth and the eighteenth centuries.

What we need in this discussion is evidence of identification

[76] Bertelli (1976).
[77] De Mauro (1976), 81ff., 96ff.
[78] Eisenstein (1979), 80–8; cf. Quondam (1983).

with 'nostra lingua'. Given what was said earlier about the importance of reactive identity, it may be useful to compare attitudes to the invasion of foreign words in different periods.

In the sixteenth and seventeenth centuries, the invasion came from Spain. Spanish administrative, legal and military terms in particular were taken into Italian in the period in which Spanish governors and viceroys ruled Milan, Naples and Sicily.[79] Needless to say, the Spaniards were not altogether popular in Italy. There were complaints about the hispanization of Italian manners, emphasizing the Spanish stress on *cerimonie* and on grandiloquent titles such as *Magnifico, Illustre* and even *Vostra Signoria*.[80]

All the same, the infiltration of Italian by Spanish words does not seem to have evoked much of a reaction. It cannot be said that this kind of linguistic consciousness was anachronistic in this period; some Frenchmen, such as the printer Henri Estienne, were already extremely well aware of, and hostile to, the penetration of French by Italianisms such as *spaceger, strade, bon garbe* or *à bastanse*, which he regarded as examples of 'this barbarous jargon called the language of courtiers' ('ce jargon si sauvage / Appelé courtisan langage').[81] Our conclusion must be that in the sixteenth and seventeenth centuries the consciousness of being Italian was not yet linked very closely to language.

In the eighteenth century, the foreign language which increasingly penetrated Italian was French. This penetration, which some modern scholars have described as a 'crisis of language', was discussed by a number of writers and intellectuals of the time.[82] Among the French words and phrases which were taken into Italian at this time were *felicitazione, madamosella, ragù, regretto, vengo di dire*. This trend evoked a variety of reactions.

On one side, there was Count Melchiorre Cesarotti, who was prepared to approve of borrowing in moderation, though even he condemned what he called 'The liberties taken by those who go round frenchifying the Italian language all the time without reason' ('la licenza di coloro che vanno tutto giorno infrancescando la lingua italiana senza proposito'). On the other side there was

[79] Beccaria (1968).
[80] Boccalini (1678), vol. 1, 38; cf. Croce (1917), esp. 148ff., 182ff.
[81] Estienne (1578), 35, 66, 72, etc.
[82] Schiaffini (1937), esp. 151ff.; Migliorini (1960), 574ff.; Vitale (1962), esp. 271ff., 285ff.; Durante (1981), 214ff.

Carlo Gozzi and Count Gianfrancesco Galeani Napioni, who totally rejected what they called 'Frenchiness' (*il francesismo*) and the 'hybrid speech' (*ermafrodita favella*) which resulted from it.[83] Cesarotti criticized his opponents as 'purists' and he was in turn criticized for his 'extreme tolerance' (*tollerantismo*).

From the point of view of the history of identity, the interest of this debate lies in the assumptions the participants made about the relation between language and nationhood. Alessandro Verri, for example, refers to 'the national language' (*la lingua nazionale*).[84] Giuseppe Baretti insisted that the language in which 'everyone born on the piece of land called Italy writes', should be described not as 'Florentine' or 'Tuscan' but as 'Italian'.[85]

Count Galeani Napioni, whose remarks on the links between language and *patria* were quoted at the beginning of the chapter, made the clearest and the most forceful statements of the link between language and that key concept of the eighteenth century, 'national character'. 'Languages are a result of the climate, the nature, the mind, the moral character, the dominant arts, the studies, the professions and the political organization of different nations' ('Le lingue sono un risultamento del clima, dell'indole, del naturale ingegno, del carattere morale, delle arti dominanti, degli studi, delle professioni, della istituzione politica delle nazioni diverse').[86] The only word lacking here was 'organic'. In the nineteenth century, many writers would rush to supply it.

To sum up. The later eighteenth century was a crucial period in the development of the association between language and national identity among Italian intellectuals. It was the time when substantial numbers of them began to speak Tuscan (or something like it), at least some of the time. It was also the time when the national language was linked to the new discovery – or is it invention? – national character. It is at this point, rather than the Renaissance, that language, rather than ritual, or myth, or material culture, came to carry the burden of identity.

---

[83]  Puppo (1957).
[84]  Ibid., 259.
[85]  Ibid., 234.
[86]  Ibid., 503, 499–500.

# 4

## The Art of Conversation in Early Modern Europe

'The art of conversation, so essentially French, of which the history is so difficult to write' (Georges Mongrédien)

'Conversation must naturally follow the spirit of the age' (Orlando Sabertash)

Older people, at least in England, often remark on the decline of the art of conversation, whether in general or in particular environments like the common rooms and combination rooms of Oxford and Cambridge. When this decline took place, where, and among whom – or indeed when it was that conversation originally 'rose' – are difficult questions for them, or indeed for anyone, to answer. The problem of decline would seem to be an appropriate subject of investigation for a social historian of language, at least when it has been 'neutralized', in other words redefined as 'change'.

It has sometimes been claimed that the art of conversation, like love and *haute cuisine*, is a French invention.[1] It will be argued here, however, that important changes in the manner and style of conversation took place in Renaissance Italy and in eighteenth-century Britain as well as in France in its 'great century'. Earlier

---

Epigraphs from Mongrédien (1947), 187, and Sabertash (1842), 33.

[1]   Deschanel (1857), 11, 25.

chapters of this book have referred in passing to the possible effect of the rise of printing on spoken as well as written language. In this case, however, the interaction of speech and print will be a major theme, discussed in the final section in particular.

## CONVERSATION AS ART

'The Art of Conversation' is the title of a number of manuals which appeared between the seventeenth and the nineteenth centuries in England, France and elsewhere.[2] They are in fact only the tip of an important iceberg – of a group of texts which, whatever their titles, tell their readers how to speak, whether generally or on particular kinds of occasion. Such texts are still being produced, but the emphasis has changed in our own century from the social to the psychological – from the art of showing oneself to be well bred to that of acquiring confidence, 'breaking the ice', and making friends.

This cluster of manuals forms a subgroup of the many treatises on good behaviour, good manners, courtesy or 'civility' printed in Europe from the fifteenth century onwards, treatises which have attracted the attention of historians, literary critics, and sociologists (notably the late Norbert Elias).[3] They have occasionally been studied from other points of view, as illustrations of the seventeenth-century interest in psychology, for example, especially the art of understanding the hidden intentions of others by paying close attention to their speech.[4]

However, these books also deserve the attention of historians, linguists and others interested in the social history of language, whether as sources helping them to reconstruct ways of speaking in particular places and times, or as documents illustrating the interaction of oral and written modes of communication. It is from this latter perspective, that of a historical ethnography of communication, that this essay has been written. Its occasion was the discovery of parallels between the cultural rules which ethnographers and linguists try to discover – who communicates with whom, when, where, about what, in what manner, and so

---

[2]  Ortigue (1688); Constable (1738); Anon (1757); Chazet (1812); Sabertash (1842); Anon (1897).
[3]  Elias (1939).
[4]  Henn-Schmölder (1975).

on – and the advice given in treatises written several centuries earlier. The systematic comparison of the two sets of rules should help to illuminate both.[5]

The question whether conversations follow 'rules' or 'principles', and in what sense such rules or principles are to be understood (strict or flexible, consciously followed or observed from outside, and so on), is currently a controversial one among linguists and philosophers alike.[6] The controversy is complicated by the fact that the participants do not always use the term 'conversation' in the same way. The pioneers of what is known as 'conversation analysis', Harvey Sacks and Emmanuel Schegloff, are concerned with verbal exchanges in general, but others treat conversation (as early modern writers did and as I shall do here) as a particular kind of speech act, speech event, or speech genre.

What makes this genre distinctive is the relative emphasis on a cluster of characteristics, four in particular. There is first 'the cooperative principle', as the philosopher H. P. Grice has called it; second, the equal distribution of 'speaker rights', expressed through the emphasis on turn-taking and what the novelist Henry Fielding called a 'reciprocal interchange of ideas'; third, the spontaneity and informality of the exchanges; and finally what one linguist calls their 'non-business-likeness', a term reminiscent of Dr Johnson's definition of conversation as 'Talk beyond that which is necessary to the purposes of actual business'.[7] The points are neatly summed up by the comparison between conversation and tennis, now commonplace but apparently new when it was formulated by the writer François La Mothe Le Vayer in the 1640s. 'Just as it is useless in handball (*au jeu de la paulme*) to strike the ball hard if it is not returned to you, so conversation cannot be pleasant if repartee is lacking.'[8]

The similarities bettween current formulations and those of earlier centuries are worth emphasizing. The main conclusion to have emerged from the contemporary debate is that the notion of 'rule' or norm must not be understood in too mechanical a fashion. In this context, as in others discussed above (p. 15), it

---

[5] Cf. Strosetzki (1978), 11.
[6] Grice (1975); Taylor and Cameron (1987); Searle (1992); Dascal (1992).
[7] Grice (1975); Wilson (1989); Fielding (1743), 123; Donaldson (1979); Johnson quoted Piozzi (1974), 74.
[8] La Mothe (1643–4), vol. 2, 228.

may better to think in terms of what Pierre Bourdieu, following Aristotle, has called 'habitus'.[9] Eighteenth-century writers were thinking in somewhat similar terms when they called conversation an 'art'.

However, early modern writers make some other points which modern theorists might do well to take into account. For example, a number of treatises discuss competition in conversation, condemning extreme forms of it but admitting the desire to 'shine'.[10] In other words, the game could be played in an 'adversarial' as well as a 'collaborative', manner.[11] If conversation is the verbal equivalent of tennis, there are some participants who play to defeat an opponent rather than to keep the ball in the air for the longest possible time.

Again, the many references to equality and reciprocity in conversation are matched by other references to the social hierarchy and marks of respect, and advice is often given about ways of speaking to one's superiors and inferiors. These references are a reminder that early modern European society was more hierarchical, and above all more openly hierarchical, than our own. The treatises have much to say about the need to include all 'the company' in the conversation, but it went without saying that this company excluded some people physically present, notably servants.

As for the references to spontaneity of speech, they are contradicted by the very existence of the treatises as well as their advice to study in order to improve conversational performance. A reading of these texts suggests that a truly general theory of conversation should discuss the tension and the balance between the competitive and cooperative principles, between equality and hierarchy, between inclusion and exclusion, and between spontaneity and study, rather than placing all the weight on the first item in each of these pairs.

## SOURCES, PROBLEMS AND METHODS

The value of the treatises on conversation to a cultural historian is that they make explicit norms which were usually implicit. Actually the last statement, obvious as it may seem, needs to be

---

[9]   Bourdieu (1972), 78.
[10]   Della Casa (1558), ch. 18; Morvan (1703), 79.
[11]   For these distinctions see Lakoff (1990), 72.

qualified. The authors of the treatises cannot be assumed to be articulating a social consensus. Different social groups within the same society may follow different rules for communication, while some authors may be subverting the rules current in their own culture. In his essays and dialogues on conversation, as in some of his other works, Jonathan Swift resorted to parody. His collection of 'Phrases Invented to Cultivate Conversation' is in fact a malicious list of clichés.[12]

Thus the manuals are far from being an unproblematic source. Indeed, at first sight, one might well think that there was nothing at all to say about these texts from the point of view of this chapter. The first problem, that of reconstructing speech from writing has already been discussed in some detail (above, p. 21), and it must be admitted that the approach adopted here involves an emphasis on just what the sources are most reluctant to tell us. To coax information about practice from treatises offering a theory of conversation means reading the texts against the grain, with all the dangers implied by that procedure.

However, the argument of the chapter does not depend on the analysis of precepts alone. The reception of the texts will also be examined, and other kinds of source utilized wherever possible to test the major hypotheses which emerge and to serve as a check on one another.

For example, the descriptions of conversational style offered by foreign travellers, although they are sometimes superficial or overly influenced by stereotypes of national character, still register significant differences between what might be called the indigenous 'speech culture' and that of the visitor. Even legal or financial documents may tell us something about speech. For example, a seventeenth-century Genoese patrician, Marcello Doria, complained of his wife's speech style (*modo di parlare*), which according to him 'broke all the rules of conversation' ('offendeva ogni termine di conversatione').[13] It is from the household accounts of Henri III of France that we learn that the king forebade people to speak to him at meals except on 'general subjects worthy of the presence of His said Majesty' ('propos communs et dignes de la présence de Sadite Majesté'), such as history and 'other matters concerning learning and virtue'.[14]

[12] Swift (1939–68), vol. 4, 106.
[13] Archivio di Stato, Genoa, fondo Brignole Sale, ms 709.
[14] Ranum (1980), 34n.

A second problem for the historian is that the manuals appear to be little more than the articulation of common sense and good manners. They are essentially a collection of commonplaces – 'don't talk about yourself', 'don't interrupt other speakers', and so on – repeated over the centuries, and thus resisting history – or at any rate historians. In a manual published in 1991, the 'don't interrupt' rule is presented as a conclusion based on empirical 'surveys' by the author, but it can be found in Cicero as well as in many of the early modern treatises to be discussed in this chapter.[15]

This second problem requires a more extended response at both the conceptual and the empirical level. As anthropologists have shown again and again, what is regarded as 'common sense' varies a good deal from culture to culture. Common sense should therefore be viewed as a 'cultural system', or part of one, in other words as what Clifford Geertz has described as 'a relatively organized body of considered thought'.[16] A similar point might be made about notions of good manners, questioning the assumption of Norbert Elias in his famous study of the subject that while different groups or cultures are more or less civilized, 'civility' is unchanging.[17]

In the case of conversational standards, anthropological and historical approaches have the advantage of defamiliarization, showing that what is taken for granted within a particular culture may not be accepted in other places and times. A linguist interested in a comparative approach recently drew attention to what he calls 'our treatment in western culture, and in particular in Anglo-Saxon culture, of violations of ordinary turn-taking practices as impoliteness or lack of civility'.[18] A visitor to Latin countries, on the other hand, soon learns that it is necessary to listen, or at least to attempt to listen, to several people speaking at the same time.

In the case of conversation as in that of good manners, it might be prudent to assume that different cultures have their own ideals, which may overlap but rarely coincide, and that the task of the historian, like that of the anthropologist or sociolinguist, is

---

[15] Glass (1991), 35; cf. Cicero (1913) 1.37; Cebà (1617) ch. 44; La Salle (1695), 182, etc.
[16] Geertz (1983).
[17] Elias (1939), esp. vol. 1, ch. 2.
[18] Schegloff (1988), 98.

to discover what these ideals were or are. One might begin by taking the cluster of early modern manuals on conversation as a problem as well as a source, and asking when, where and for whom they were written.

As for the empirical question of the recurrence of commonplaces, a closer study of the manuals reveals small yet significant changes over time, especially over the long term, changes in emphasis or 'inflections' which are well worth the attention of historians of language and social behaviour.[19] A recent handbook to successful conversation rejects the advice offered by a relatively recent predecessor, Dale Carnegie, as out-of-date 'Depression-era teachings'.[20] If changes in standards are so obvious after fifty years, they should also be worth investigating over the centuries.

Before such an investigation can start, an apparently simple question is in order. What exactly was the contemporary notion of 'conversation'? In early modern Europe, the term was used in several languages with a wider range of meanings than is usual today, while our verb 'to converse' might be rendered in Italian by *ragionare*, in French by *deviser*.[21] The first treatise to use the word 'conversation' in its title, Stefano Guazzo's *La civil conversazione* (1574) is a general discussion of social relations in which speaking plays only a part – though an important one.

In the late classical Latin of Seneca, *conversatio* meant something like 'intimacy'. This usage can also be found in vernacular languages in the early modern period. Thus an Italian treatise recommends fleeing the *conversatione*, that is the company, of vicious people.[22] In Italian, at least in the eighteenth century, *conversazione* might refer to an assembly or party. The Italian term was occasionally used in England at the time and still survives in some circles today (at least in the Royal Society).

Again, when Nicolas Faret's *Honnête homme* uses the term *conversation*, which it does quite frequently, it is usually if not always to refer to social relationships.[23] James Cleland's treatise on the gentleman also includes under the concept of 'civil conversation' the company a young man should keep. In similar fashion

[19] Cf. Foucault (1984), 50.
[20] Glass (1991), 40.
[21] Lievsay (1961), 34ff.; Auernheimer (1973), 27ff.
[22] Trotto (1578).
[23] Faret (1630), 56, 64, 68, 88.

the action for 'criminal conversation', an important means of
dissolving marriages in early modern England, was concerned not
with talk but with extramarital intimacies.[24] All the same, since
it is difficult to imagine either intimacy or assemblies without
speech, there is much to learn about forms of talk from these
texts.

## CLASSICAL AND MEDIEVAL TRADITIONS

The point of departure for this study will be Renaissance Italy.
This choice implies no assumption that interest in conversation
(let alone sophisticated speech) was lacking in earlier periods.
Among the Greeks, Socrates was presented by Plato as a master
of the art of speaking or of encouraging others to speak in small
groups. Plutarch wrote one treatise on garrulity and how to cure
it, and another, the *Symposiakon*, on the appropriate topics of
conversation at *symposia* or drinking parties, including philosophy
but excluding idle, frivolous, empty talk.[25] Dio Chrysostom also
discussed *symposia*, praising the man who 'introduces appropriate
topics of conversation' there 'in order to create harmony'.[26]

Among the Romans, Cicero discussed what he calls 'ordinary
talk' (*sermo communis*) in his treatise on social duties, noting
that – unlike public oratory – the rules of private conversation
have not been formulated. He recommended that talk of this
kind be free from the passions and easy-going (*lenis*); that it
include everyone and allow everyone to take his turn; and that it
should avoid malicious gossip about people who are not present.[27]

The Roman scholar Varro also discussed talk at dinner parties,
and was in turn discussed by Aulus Gellius, whose ideal 'urbane
man' (*urbanus homo*) was interested in conversation.[28] These
classical texts were well known in the early modern period.
Indeed, it would not be very much of an exaggeration to describe
the manuals discussed below as a series of footnotes to Cicero.

[24]  Cleland (1607); Stone (1992), 221–30.
[25]  On Socrates, Ramage (1973), 10–11; Plutarch (1927–69), vol. 6, 395–467, and vol.
10, esp. book 8.
[26]  Dio (1939), vol. 2, 351 (the 27th discourse).
[27]  Cicero (1913), 1.37; cf. Ramage (1973), 58–64.
[28]  Aulus Gellius (1927), 13.11.

In the Middle Ages, on the other hand, there seems to be no real equivalent to classical or modern discussions of ordinary conversation. This is not to say that skill in different forms of talk was not taken seriously. Among the troubadours, Marcabru refers to the decorum (*mesura*) of 'polite talk' (*gent parlar*).[29] Further north, in what we now call Germany, what was called *urbanitas* was much appreciated in court circles.[30] In his famous treatise on courtly love, Andreas Capellanus provides model speeches for men and women of different social status to make to one another.[31] Medieval romances refer from time to time to conversation in different styles or on different topics, especially to stylized flirtation or 'dalliance'.[32] Indeed, it has been suggested that in the later Middle Ages, 'The importance of talk in the aristocratic, ideal world of courtly living can hardly be exaggerated.'[33]

Not only is this talk lost, however, but little seems to be known about its style, its rules or conventions. Unlike later references to *bien parler* or *badinage*, medieval allusions to *urbanitas* or *gent parlar* or dalliance are not amplified by detailed descriptions. Although a number of manuals on good behaviour, 'courtesy books' as we call them, were produced in the later Middle Ages, they have little to say about speech. Rules were formulated for the clergy, especially monks, but they tended not to go beyond the general and rather vague recommendation to avoid the extremes of garrulity and taciturnity.[34] Even the thirteenth-century treatise 'on speech and silence' by the Italian writer Albertanus is concerned mainly with public speaking.[35] A general idea or ideal of conversation in different situations and on different topics seems to have been lacking, and even the techniques of dalliance were left implicit. From the Middle Ages, all that remains are fragments overheard, tantalizing echoes of the speech conventions of the period.

In contrast, the age of print is also the age of a proliferation of manuals discussing how to talk on various kinds of occasions,

[29]   Marcabru (1909), poem no. xv.
[30]   Jaeger (1985), 145ff.
[31]   Capellanus (1941).
[32]   Tolkien and Gordon (1925), line 1012.
[33]   Stevens (1961), 159.
[34]   Casagrande and Vecchi (1987).
[35]   Albertanus (1507).

public and private. The manuals cluster in three regions, Italy, France and Britain, in the sixteenth, seventeenth and eighteenth centuries respectively. Attention will therefore be focussed on these three geographical areas and these three 'moments' in particular (excluding Spanish texts, from Palmireno to Feijóo, and German ones, from Sagittarius to Knigge, despite their intrinsic interest).[36] The texts to be discussed are listed in chronological order in the appendix to this chapter.

## SIXTEENTH-CENTURY ITALY

According to the poet Giacomo Leopardi, Italians do not care for conversation. This deliberately shocking statement was not, of course, a claim that Italians dislike talking. On the contrary, it was a criticism of the aggressively competitive style of speaking in vogue in Leopardi's day, 'nothing but a pure and continuous war without truce' ('non altra che una pura e continua guerra senza tregua'), and a plea for showing more respect to other participants in dialogue.[37]

The Italians also like to talk about talk, and they seem to have done this with particular vigour in the sixteenth century, when the *questione della lingua*, the question whether 'high' Italian should or should not follow Florentine usage, was at its height.[38] A concern with the diversity of speech and with its place in social life also seems to have become particularly acute during the Renaissance, when it was exemplified by major and minor writers alike.[39] It was surely no accident that the adjectives *conversabile* and *conversativo*, meaning both 'sociable' and 'talkative', are first recorded in texts from this period. One famous Renaissance dialogue on language listed no fewer than eight terms referring to what we might call 'small talk': *cicalare, ciarlare, cinguettare, cingottare, ciangolare, ciaramellare, chiacchierare* and *cornacchiare*.[40] As to the style of this small talk, it is often

---

[36]  Palmireno (1577); Gracián (1646); Feijóo (1781); Sagittarius (1603); Harsdörffer (1641–9); Knigge (1788).
[37]  Leopardi (1824), 865.
[38]  Bembo (1525); Varchi (1570); Hall (1942); Vitale (1962).
[39]  Bembo (1525); Borghini (1971); Cebà (1617); Giustinelli (1609); Politiano (1547); Varchi (1570).
[40]  Varchi (1570), 42.

suggested that it should be 'witty' (*motteggievole*) and even 'biting' (*mordace*). One famous text refers to 'the sweetness of victory' ('la dolcezza di vincere') as one of the pleasures of conversation, confirming the justice of Leopardi's complaint about the adversarial style of his fellow-countrymen.[41]

Three Italian treatises were pre-eminent both for the attention they devoted to the topic of conversation and for their importance in their own time, as measured by numbers of editions: Castiglione's (*Cortegiano* (1528), Della Casa's *Galateo* (1558) and Guazzo's *Civil conversazione* (1574).

Castiglione makes an especially appropriate point of departure because his dialogue – to a much greater extent than most Renaissance dialogues – is presented in the form of a stylized conversation, including informal interruptions and the teasing of participants as well as oratorical set-pieces. Looking backwards from the later treatises, Castiglione's recommendations on conversation may seem somewhat jejune, squeezed between a detailed account of physical exercises and the problem of the best form of Italian for courtiers to speak and write. Only speaking to princes is presented as problematic. On the other hand, unlike earlier treatises on courtly behaviour, such as Diomede Caraffa's *Dello optimo cortesano* (*c.*1479), which does little more than extol the virtues of silence, Castiglione's *Courtier* devotes considerable attention to witty and gracious everyday speech.[42] In this as in other respects the author follows the model of Cicero, to whom he pays explicit homage at the beginning of his book, but he illustrates his precepts in the conversations represented in the dialogue itself.

In the first book of *The Courtier*, Count Lodovico da Canossa declares that the grace required of the ideal courtier is shown 'most of all in his speech' ('massimamente nel parlare'). More specifically, he recommends aspiring courtiers to avoid affectation in speaking, indiscreet joking and also self-praise.[43] In the second book, Federico Fregoso recommends 'a kind and friendly style of everyday conversation' ('una gentile ed amabile manera nel conversare cottidiano'), including the ability to shift styles – 'registers', as the linguists say today – in order to choose one appropriate for the other participants. The courtier is praised for being witty

[41] Della Casa (1558), ch. 18.
[42] Carafa (1971), chs 17–18.
[43] Castiglione (1528), 1.17–18, 1.22, 1.28; cf. Hinz (1992), 103–9.

and skilled at repartee ('arguto e pronto nelle risposte').[44] Fregoso also recommends enlivening conversation with jokes, thus arousing a debate illustrated with many examples.[45]

In the third book of *The Courtier*, Giuliano de' Medici suggests that ladies too ought to be able to converse, and indeed to joke, with 'every kind of man'. In this case, however, there is a conflict between theory and practice in the sense that the ladies are represented in Castiglione's dialogue as playing an extremely muted role, despite the fact that the Duchess of Urbino is the person of highest status present and that Lady Emilia Pia chairs the discussion. Their relative silence appears all the more significant when we learn that in earlier drafts of the dialogue Castiglione gave ladies more speaking parts. Margherita Gonzaga, for example, was originally allowed to initiate a new topic of conversation, but this passage was later deleted by the author.[46]

One of Castiglione's characters remarked that – as recent linguists have reiterated – the idea of conversation implies a kind of equality ('questo nome di conversare importi una certa parità'), and exchange on an equal basis informs the whole dialogue.[47] In order to make this plausible, Castiglione had to set his dialogue in a court without a ruler – for the duke, a dying man, is represented as reposing in his chamber while the conversations are taking place. Hierarchy reappears when the participants discuss the way in which a courtier should talk to his prince, or more exactly how he should not talk to his prince. He should not be offensive, should not boast, should not contradict, and so on. Recent scholarship has shown that the emphasis on hierarchy is stronger in the published version of the text than it was in earlier drafts.[48]

In some respects Della Casa's *Galateo*, which devotes about a third of its space to conversation, reads like an amplification of Castiglione's remarks on the subject, simplified for the sake of a wider audience. Della Casa too knows his Cicero – indeed, he wrote a treatise on duties, *De officiis inter potentiores et tenuiores amicos*, which pays homage to Cicero in its very title. Della

---

[44] Castiglione (1528), 2.32.
[45] Ibid., 2.42–83.
[46] Guidi (1980).
[47] Castiglione (1528), 2.18; cf. Donaldson (1979).
[48] Castiglione (1528), 2.17–18; Guidi (1983).

Casa's recommendation to his readers to be 'friendly and sweet in conversation' ('amichevole e dolce nel conversare') is not far from Castiglione's 'gentile ed amabile manera'.[49]

All the same, a certain difference in tone soon becomes apparent. Della Casa is more negative and more hierarchical. Where Castiglione stressed equal exchanges, Della Casa is more concerned with unequals, in his *Galateo* as well as in his treatise on the duties of 'more powerful' and 'less powerful' friends (in other words patrons and clients).

Castiglione, or his characters, are concerned above all with the positive qualities of the ideal courtier. Della Casa, by contrast, emphasises the negative side. Chapters 11 to 13 of his treatise, which introduce the theme of speech, offer little more than a list of subjects to avoid, notably talking about one's children, telling one's dreams, or boasting of one's nobility or riches. Chapter 18 warns the reader not to contradict or correct what others have said, while the following chapter is essentially concerned with the dangers of jokes and the limits to jesting (anticipating Leopardi's complaints about conversation as a form of aggression).

Although the two books often condemn the same faults, the difference in tone between them is so great that one feels transported from the Renaissance to the Counter-Reformation. Della Casa was indeed a generation younger than Castiglione. Like him he was a poet, a papal nuncio and a friend of Bembo. Unlike Castiglione, he was actively involved with the repression of heresy, the Inquisition and the Index. Where Castiglione chose the dialogue form and allowed major differences of opinion to become apparent, Della Casa simply told his readers what and what not to do.

The third major Italian writer on conversation was Stefano Guazzo, a gentleman from Piedmont. He had the sharpest ear of the three for differences in styles of speaking according to regions, groups (such as the French Calvinists), or occasions (above, pp. 3, 11). As for his recommendations, apart from the customary warnings not to interrupt others and not to speak of oneself, they may be summed up in two words, *accommodazione* and *mediocrità*. The latter term sums up the recommendation (which had the authority of Aristotle behind it) to follow the golden mean, navigating between affability and gravity, between

---

[49] Della Casa (1558); cf. Hinz (1992), 308–11.

the need to amuse and the equal need not to give offence, and so on.[50] This adherence to the *via media* helps explain the popularity of his treatise but makes it less quotable than most of the texts discussed here.

At times, however, the compromise between conflicting forces is more apparent than real. The fourth book of Guazzo's treatise, representing a social occasion at which a prince, Vespasiano Gonzaga, is present, presents a picture of hierarchy masked by an idiom of equality. Vespasiano insists on being treated like everyone else, but all the same it is he who both 'sets the subjects of conversation' and 'controls its duration'.[51]

As for 'accommodation', it may be defined as sensitivity to situation, a subject of considerable interest among linguists today. It reflected an awareness of the need to adapt or adjust one's conversation to the listeners – old or young, nobles or commoners, learned or ignorant, clergy or laity, men or women.[52]

## SEVENTEENTH-CENTURY FRANCE

These Italian texts were quite well known in other parts of Europe. Castiglione's *Courtier*, for example, was translated into French and Spanish in the 1530s, and later into Latin, English, German and Polish, By 1620 more than fifty editions of the text had appeared in languages other than Italian. By the early seventeenth century, Della Casa had been translated into German, Spanish, and twice into Latin, and Guazzo into English, Latin, Dutch and twice into French.

To judge by the frequency with which they reprinted these texts, it was the French who were most interested in the Italian model of courtly behaviour and conversation. The term *conversable*, on the model of *conversabile*, came into use in this period to describe this ideal, which was discussed in print in France with increasing frequency.[53] It was treated as an important part of good behaviour in Eustache du Refuge's *Traité de la cour* (1617); in the anonymous *Maximes de la bienséance en la conversation*

[50]   Guazzo (1574), 100ff.: cf. Hinz (1992), part v.
[51]   Whigham (1984), 108.
[52]   Guazzo (1574), 108ff.
[53]   Dens (1973); Strosetzki (1978).

(1618), which apparently originated at the Jesuit college of La Flèche, and includes forty maxims to do with speaking in company; in Nicolas Faret's *L'honnête homme* (1630), an imitation of *The Courtier* which also drew on Della Casa and Guazzo; and in Jacques du Bosc's *Honnête femme* (1632). Of these works the most influential seems to have been the *Maximes*. It was translated into Latin, English and Czech, and continued to be used as late as the mid-eighteenth century and as far afield as colonial America, where a schoolboy named George Washington wrote out a paraphrase of its recommendations in the form of fifty-seven rules of behaviour.[54]

Later in the century, the tradition was carried on by Antoine Courtin's *Nouvelle traité de la civilité* (1671), plagiarized by François de Fenne's *Entretiens familiers* (1690); Joachim Trotti de la Chetardye's *Instructions pour un jeune seigneur* (1683); Jean-Baptiste de La Salle's *Les règles de la bienséance* (1695); and Antoine Renaud's *Manière de parler* (1697). Like the *Maximes* of 1618, La Salle's treatise was intended for schoolboys. For adults, there were the sections on conversation in the Duc de La Rochefoucauld's *Réflexions diverses* (composed in the 1670s but only published after the author's death in 1680). Unlike the same author's more famous *Réflexions morales*, these remarks on conversation were not intended to shock but simply to articulate the conventional wisdom in a refined and subtle manner. There was also the chapter in La Bruyère's *Caractères* (1688), a savage description of the worst faults of conversation, distilled into a few biting paragraphs.

Treatises on correct language, which were numerous, are also relevant here, because the use of 'polite' or 'polished' language, avoiding barbarisms, solecisms, and so on, was a necessary condition for good conversation, as for good manners or – to use the fashionable word of the age – *galanterie*. The most important of these discussions, from our point of view, are Claude Favre de Vaugelas' *Remarques sur la langue française* (1647) and Dominique Bouhours' *Remarques nouvelles sur la langue française* (1675). The term 'remarks', incidentally, was chosen by these two authors precisely because they believed that 'laws' were inappropriate in this domain. All the same, they were both ex-

---

[54] Washington (1886).

tremely firm in their rejection of dialect, technical terms, 'low' words and what they called 'dishonourable words' (*mots deshonnêtes*), including in their number some words for parts of the body, such as *poitrine* ('bosom').[55]

That these ideas were taken seriously by some ladies at least is suggested by the fact that Molière poked fun at them on two occasions, in his *Précieuses ridicules* (1659) and again in his *Femmes savantes* (1672). In the first play, Cathos and Magdelon criticize what they call 'vulgar' speech and are in turn criticized by their father for what he calls 'jargon', while the learned ladies in the second play cannot bear to hear expressions condemned by Vaugelas.[56] As sociolinguists point out, 'hypercorrectness' has been especially characteristic of women (above, p. 9).

That the reading public in France was becoming more interested in this topic in the mid-seventeenth century is also suggested by the presentation of the new translations of Castiglione and Guazzo, both by the Abbé Duhamel. His version of *Il Galateo*, published in 1666, was subtitled 'l'art de plaire dans la conversation', while his *Cortegiano* was described on the title-page as 'useful for suceess in elegant conversations' ('avantageux pour réussir dans les belles conversations').

To this new interest we owe the rise of a new genre, the treatise or dialogue devoted completely to conversation in the precise sense of the term. The most important of these were René Bary's *L'esprit de cour, ou les conversations galantes* (1662), the Chevalier de Méré's *Discours de la conversation* (1677), Pierre Ortigue de Vaumorière's *L'art de plaire dans la conversation* (1688), and Jean-Baptiste Morvan de Bellegarde's *Modèles de conversations pour les personnes polies* (1697). Bary, for example, presented his ideas in the form of a dialogue or conversation in which the participants discuss (among other subjects) the language of compliment, the art of teasing and flirting (*raillerie, badinage, coquetterie*), and so on.

Even religious writers were affected by the trend. The anonymous *Méthode pour converser avec Dieu* (1679) presented prayer in the form of a familiar conversation. There is even more to be found, paradoxically enough, in the rules for the most silent of

[55]    Brunot (1905–), vol. 3, part 2, chs 3–6.
[56]    Molière (1962), 11–13, 539–40.

monasteries, La Trappe, especially for their *conférences*, in other words their rare but compulsory intervals of speech. One might have expected the rules for monks to be very different from those of the laity, but they too followed the laws of 'civil conversation', while adding a few precepts of their own.

In a brief account it is obviously out of the question to summarize each of these texts separately or to attempt to assess what each author contributed to the common stock. It is this common stock of 'common sense' which will be the focus of attention. It is most easily summarized in the form of a list of 'do's and don'ts', a form of presentation which is followed by some of the treatises themselves.[57]

This cluster of treatises shows many continuities with the conversational tradition. Faret, for example, follows his Italian models in warning the reader not to talk too much, while Trotti declares that 'people who speak a good deal . . . are not suitable for the court.'[58] Faret, the Chevalier de Méré and Morvan de Bellegarde all recommend the 'accommodation' of one's conversation to the company. As the last of these writers put it, 'the greatest secret of conversation is to relate it to the kind of company one keeps' ('le plus grand secret de la Conversation est de se proportionner au caractère des personnes que l'on frequente').[59]

This apparently bland assertion was probably a reference to the need to behave differently to people with different positions in the social hierarchy, a point made explicit in Courtin's treatise on civility. An inferior referring to a superior should not say 'he told me' but 'he did me the honour of telling me.' He should not provide the word which has escaped his superior, and he should not be the first to reply to a question when people of higher status are present.[60]

Never recount your dreams in public, the *Maximes* and La Salle warn their readers, echoing Della Casa. Indeed, it is 'uncivil' to speak about oneself all the time.[61] The point is made still more strongly, for obvious reasons, in the Trappist rules: 'On ne parlera jamais du soi, ni en bien ni en mal.' Indeed, 'one will rarely offer

[57]  Anon (1618). cf. Anon (1775), 82–9; Trusler (1775); Morellet (1812), 86ff.
[58]  Faret (1630), 73–7; Trotti (1683), 35.
[59]  Faret (1630), 47; Méré (1677), 106; Morvan (1697), 'avertissement'. Cf. Ortigue (1688), 18.
[60]  Courtin (1671).
[61]  Anon (1618), ch. 7, no. 1; La Rochefoucauld (1946), 154; La Salle (1695), 169.

one's own opinion, but repeat those of the saints' ('On dira rarement ses propres pensées, mais on rapportera celles des Saints').[62]

Interruption was still a sin. 'Two people will never speak at a time. The younger monks will have the good grace to speak less than the others.' Secular writers also told their readers not to interrupt. 'It is necessary to wait one's turn' ('il faut attendre à parler que son tour soit venu').[63] They also reiterated the need to listen and the traditional warning against monopolizing the conversation. 'It is necessary to listen to others if one wants to have their attention.'[64] 'Conversation is not like making speeches [La conversation n'est pas de la nature des Harangues]. Everyone should listen and speak in turn.' The familiar style of conversation excludes 'the imperious tone' (*le ton impérial*) and a 'decisive, assertive manner' (*l'air décisif et affirmatif*).[65]

Like Castiglione, Ortigue recommends his readers to avoid affectation and recommends a manner which he declares to be 'more or less the equivalent of the urbanity of the ancient Romans'.[66] The need for at least apparent spontaneity in conversation, a fundamental rule of the genre, is stressed again and again. The authors of the *Maximes* tell their readers to avoid 'subtleties' and figures of speech. Sorel recommends hesitation and even an occasional clumsiness in order to preserve the illusion of spontaneity. Méré warns against speaking 'too well', others against speech which is 'eloquent', or a manner which is 'constrained', or 'studied', when it should be 'free', 'natural', and 'easy' (*facile, aisé*). For this reason it is better to follow 'instinct' (in other words, the 'habitus') rather than 'rules'.[67]

In some cases, however, inflections in the treatment of a traditional topic are clues to wider changes in attitude and in practice. As one might have expected in the age of the salons, there is more concern with the proper way to speak to women, including a little flattery.[68] Wit was now treated with more caution than it

[62] Anon (1719), 56.
[63] Ibid., 57; La Salle (1695), 179, 182; cf. Anon (1618), ch. 7, no. 13.
[64] La Rochefoucauld (1946), 154.
[65] Trotti (1683), 38; Ortigue (1688), 64, 94ff.; Renaud (1697), 149.
[66] Ortigue (1688), 270, 272.
[67] Anon (1618), ch. 7, no. 12; Sorel quoted in Strosetzki (1978), 36; Méré (1677), 106, 109; Trotti (1683), 38; Ortigue (1688), 270; Morvan (1697), 'avertissement'.
[68] Méré (1677), 124.

had been in Castiglione's day. Du Refuge, for instance, tempered his praise of 'facility in replies' with a remark about the need to avoid 'brusque and bitter repartee' ('les rudes et aigres reparties'). Faret's long discussion of the dangers of mockery and wit (*raillerie, bons mots*) also suggests that he was less happy with jesting than his Italian predecessors had been. Later writers added objections to various kinds of joke, such as gibes, clowning and puns (*quolibets, turlupinades, équivoques*), associating them with the common people or at best with the bourgeoisie.[69] Despite the continuing references to the need to 'season' the conversation with jokes and make it more 'piquant', the treatises recommended their readers to take care what they said in order to distinguish themselves from their social inferiors.[70]

Swearing was rejected for similar reasons. Self-control, 'prudence' and 'discretion' were recommended as well as, or in spite of, the cultivation of spontaneity. The withdrawal of the elite from popular culture had affected conversational style.[71] Low words should be confined to low people. 'Honourable people must never use a low word in their speech' ('jamais les honnêtes gens ne doivent en parlant user d'un mot bas').[72]

New recommendations and prohibitions made change in the system even more apparent, and included the subjects of conversation as well as speaking style. Some writers, beginning with La Rochefoucauld, distinguished 'serious' conversation in academies and elsewhere from what they call *conversation enjouée* or *galante*, adjectives which might be translated as 'light' conversation.[73]

Conflict rather than consensus marked recommendations on the proper topics of conversation. On the one hand, the author of a conduct-book for women remarked that they are tired of male visitors who talk of nothing but 'hunting, and hawking, and the wars of the Netherlands'. On the other, women were told to avoid the subjects of fashionable clothes and 'housewifery'.[74] Trotti advised that the subjects of conversation should be 'indifferent matters', thus excluding religion and politics, which

---

69 Du Refuge (1617), 8, 10; Faret (1630), 81ff.; Méré (1677), 115–16; Ortigue (1688), 44, 212, 272; Morvan (1697), quoted Strosetzki (1978), 31; Renaud (1697), 153.
70 Renaud (1697), 146–7.
71 Burke (1978), 270–80.
72 Vaugelas (1647), 123.
73 La Rochefoucauld (1950), 28; Irson (1662), 209.
74 Du Bosc (1632).

often gave rise to disputes, while Mlle de Scudéry recommended everyday and light topics ('de choses ordinaires et galantes'), rather than serious ones ('de grandes choses').[75] Faced with this array of prohibitions, readers might be forgiven for wondering what was left to talk about. The result, as Vauvenargues remarked in the mid-eighteenth century, was that conversation tended to be confined to general topics, 'for the most part extremely frivolous'.[76]

The most recurrent theme, however, was the need to avoid forms of speech which were considered either too direct or excessively pedantic or technical. Direct interrogation, 'Where have you been?' for example, was discouraged, together with imperatives, and short answers such as 'Yes' and (above all) 'No'. Euphemisms (*termes plus doux*) and circumlocutions (such as 'I dare say') were recommended in order to diminish the danger of disputes.[77]

Still more extensive was the list of new prohibitions. It was now considered uncivil, for instance, 'to speak to someone... in a language which is not understood by the rest of the company'.[78] In similar fashion, learning, or pedantry, was excluded from polite conversation just as technical terms were excluded from polite language. Du Bosc's advice to ladies was to avoid behaving like the learned women who 'will say all, even to the marginal notes'.[79] Again, the maxims which earlier generations had learned by heart in order to impress were no longer in demand. On the contrary, the 'sententious tone' was now to be avoided.[80] At the end of the period, there are even a few signs of a reaction against ceremoniousness. Morvan de Bellegarde, for instance, once remarked that 'old-fashioned people are more formal (*formalistes*); nowadays people prefer a little more liberty.'[81]

## EIGHTEENTH-CENTURY BRITAIN

These French debates were followed with some interest in seventeenth-century England, as translations show. The *Maximes*

---

[75] Trotti (1683), 38; Scudéry (1680), 38–9.
[76] Vauvenargues (1968), vol. 1, 196–7.
[77] Courtin (1671), 50, 54; La Rochefoucauld (1946), 154; Ortigue (1688), 64; La Salle (1695), 177–9, 189.
[78] Courtin (1671), 49; cf. Anon (1618), ch. 7, no. 18.
[79] Du Bosc (1632).
[80] Méré (1677), 119; cf. Anon (1618), ch. 7, no. 1.
[81] Morvan (1703), 44.

of 1618 were translated by Francis Hawkins, and went through at least ten editions in the course of the century, under the title *Youths Behaviour, or Decency in Conversation amongst Men.* An adaptation of the treatise by Du Refuge was published as *The Art of Complaisance, or the Means to Oblige in Conversation* (1677), while the dialogues of Mademoiselle de Scudéry appeared in English in 1683.

Seventeenth-century Englishmen made their own small contribution to the subject. Bacon's *Essays* included a discussion 'of Discourse'. James Cleland devoted a chapter to the problem of 'How a Noble man should speake' in his *Heropaideia* (1607). Richard Allestree's *The Lady's Calling* (1673) included advice on 'discourse', while Locke gave the topic of conversation some attention in *Some Thoughts concerning Education* (1693).

It was, however, in the eighteenth century that this trickle became a stream, coinciding with the rise of a new kind of portrait which contemporaries, such as Richard Steele and Horace Walpole, were already calling the 'conversation-piece' (the French painted conversation also came into fashion in the early eighteenth century, and one of Watteau's paintings was already known as *La conversation* by 1733).[82] It was also at this time that some British writers proposed the foundation of an academy which would set linguistic standards on the French model, while an anonymous writer published *Remarks on the English Language* (1770). 'In the Nature of Vaugelas's Remarks on the French', as the title-page puts it, 'Being a Detection of many improper expressions used in conversation'. The English version of Ortigue, entitled *The Art of Pleasing in Conversation* and attributed, for some reason, to Cardinal Richelieu, passed through at least four editions between 1691 and 1736. As one English writer admitted, 'it will be hard to find any where more agreeable conversation, than among the French.'[83] All the same, English precepts diverged from the French in significant respects, as we shall see.

Eighteenth-century English contributors to the theory of conversation included some of the major literary figures of the time. Addison and Steele returned to the theme again and again in the pages of *The Spectator*. Swift made two major contributions, the

---

[82] Vidal (1992), 20, 67, a book which offers a view of the history of conversation from an unusual angle.
[83] Constable (1738), 89.

*Hints* and the *Polite Conversation*. Fielding was the author of an 'Essay' on the subject. Lord Chesterfield's letters to his son made frequent remarks on the topic, like Adam Petrie (later known as 'the Scottish Chesterfield') in his book on deportment. Anonymous texts such as *The Conversation of Gentlemen* (1738), attributed to J. Constable, and *The Art of Conversation* (1757), a dialogue between 'Sir Samuel Fashion', 'Sir William Civil', 'Lady Air' and others, should not be forgotten. Finally, Boswell's *Life of Johnson* (1791) not only recorded the master's pronouncements on a subject which fascinated him, but represented this 'tremendous converser' (as he was described by an acquaintance) in action, indeed in mid-dialogue.[84]

Like the letters and diaries of the period, these texts bear witness to a public interest in conversation.[85] So do contributions to the growing literature of 'politeness' – *The Polite Philosopher* (1734), *The Polite Student* (1748), *The Polite Lady* (1775) and so on. If the English were not increasingly 'conversable' (a term they had adopted from French), it was not for want of trying. Britain may not have displaced France as a model for conversation in other parts of Europe, but Chesterfield's letters, at least, were translated into French and German within a year or two of their original publication, while the Abbé Morellet, in 1812, began his essay on conversation by quoting Swift.[86]

Many of the precepts put forward in eighteenth-century England were traditional ones, and these may be dealt with briefly. Raillery, for instance, must be kept within bounds because it is a 'disturbance' to conversation. It is only acceptable if gentle and goodnatured.[87] Direct contradiction was forbidden, and indirect expressions of dissent recommended. It seems to have been in the eighteenth century that the characteristically English expression of apology 'I'm afraid that' (which foreigners still find either puzzling or amusing) came into general use. The traditional theory of 'accommodation' was reiterated. 'It is civil in Conversation to accommodate ourselves to the Company.' 'Adapt your conversation to the people you are conversing with.' Egotism, boasting

---

[84] Piozzi (1974), 128; Johnson's pronouncements in Boswell (1934), esp. vol. 2, 399, 443–4; vol. 3, 41, 57; vol. 4, 90, 186.
[85] Matthews (1936–7), 494.
[86] Morellet (1812), vol. 4, 71.
[87] Locke (1693), 201; Bond (1965), vol. 3, 582; Fielding (1743), 155.

and 'self-panegyric' continued to be banned. 'Above all things, and upon all occasions, avoid speaking of yourself.'[88] The imperious or 'positive' tone was condemned. 'Being over confident and peremptory . . . does very much unfit men for conversation.'[89]

Interrupting competitors and hogging the conversation were rejected in the traditional manner, 'the monopolizing of discourse being one of the greatest assumings imaginable, and so rude an imposing upon the company, that there can scarce be a greater indecency in conversation'. After all, 'Conversation is a sort of Bank, in which all who compose it have their respective shares.'[90] 'It is an impertinent and unreasonable Fault in Conversation, for one Man to take up all the Discourse.' 'Beware of speaking more than comes to your Share.' 'Break not in upon another's Discourse.' 'A well-bred man . . . will not take more of the discourse than falls to his share.'[91] Chesterfield also warned against holding listeners by the button so that they could not escape, a practice later known as 'button-holing'.[92]

Readers were still told to avoid foreign languages and 'syllogisms', 'Theatre-expressions, or French words', warned against 'Cant-terms', including the 'Pedantry of the Dog-Kennel and Stables', as well as that of the university and the law, and advised to choose subjects 'levelled to the capacity of the whole company'.[93] 'Never seem wiser or more learned than the company you are in.'[94] The phrase to 'talk shop' is not recorded in English until 1814, but the idea behind it is much older.

The area in which the English theory of conversation diverged most sharply from its Italian and French counterparts was that of ceremony and compliment. At the beginning of the seventeenth century, James Cleland had already recommended noblemen to speak in a 'souldier-like' manner, in other words plainly and directly. Locke warned against flattery and 'excess of Ceremony'.[95]

It is, however, in the eighteenth century, when even the French were taking a few steps in this direction, that one finds most

[88] Petrie (1720), 57; Forrester (1734), 35; Chesterfield (1774), 75, 78.
[89] Allestree (1674), 188.
[90] Allestree (1673), 7; Forrester (1734), 33.
[91] Bond (1965), vol. 4, 4; Petrie (1720), 61–2; Fielding (1743), 150.
[92] Chesterfield (1774); OED sv 'button-hole'.
[93] Petrie (1720), 57–8; Constable (1738), 46, 96, 137; Fielding (1743), 151.
[94] Trusler (1775), no. 35.
[95] Cleland (1607), 185; Locke (1693), 203.

stress on informality. Addison claimed that conversation used to be 'too stiff, formal and precise', and wanted a 'Reformation', which he compared to the Protestant Reformation in the sense that it was a reaction against excessive ceremony. His colleague Steele lamented 'the great and general want of Sincerity in Conversation', as opposed to 'The old English Plainness'. 'The Dialect of Conversation' (Steele's equivalent for our term 'register') 'is now-a-days so swell'd with Vanity and Compliment and so surfeited (as I may say) of Expressions of Kindness and Respect.'[96] Warnings were given against long apologies or excuses, for instance when one's opinion is requested.[97] The balance between equality (among members of the speech community) and hierarchy was shifting in favour of the former, at a time when even kings prided themselves on being the first gentlemen of their respective nations.

The observations of foreign visitors – notably a Swiss, who should have been neutral – confirm the contrast between the English and the French styles of conversation in this respect, with frankness (not to say rudeness) on one side, and courtesy (or was it flattery?) on the other.[98] The most vivid illustration of the English rejection of ceremony is surely the fact that Dr Johnson, an incorrigible breaker of the no-contradiction rule, should have been admired for his conversational skills. Yet Boswell hung on every word, Burke, Goldsmith and Reynolds enjoyed his company, Hogarth declared that Johnson's conversation 'was to the talk of other men, like Titian's paintings compared to Hudson's', and Mrs Piozzi that 'No man conversed so well as he upon every subject.'[99] Where else but in England could that growly bear, whom even his friends chided for his 'roughness' of manner and his silences, have achieved such a reputation?

## CONVERSATION IN SOCIAL CONTEXT

Arranging the manuals of conversation in series over nearly three centuries has the advantage of throwing changes of emphasis into

---

[96]    Bond (1965), vol. 1, 430–1, 488.
[97]    Trusler (1775), no. 18.
[98]    Muralt (1728), 230.
[99]    Piozzi (1974), 92, 97, 101, 106, 128, 139.

high relief, notably what might be called the 'feminization' of conversational standards in seventeenth-century France, and the rise of informality (or more exactly, of less formal forms) in eighteenth-century England. This 'serial' approach, as the French call it, is indispensable to a social history of conversation, but it is not of course sufficient by itself. To explain the changes it is necessary to look beyond the treatises at the social history of the time, and to do this at two different levels.

At the 'macro level', the grand scale, the rise of rules of conversation to 'control our speech and silence' ('régler notre parler et notre silence'), as Du Refuge put it, would seem to be part of wider cultural changes, such as the rise of classicism in the arts.[100] In Rome in the High Renaissance, the same circle of friends included Pietro Bembo, who laid down rules for literature as well as language, Castiglione, whose *Courtier* was read as a collection of rules for good behaviour, and Raphael, whose artistic practice became exemplary for later generations. In seventeenth-century France, the authoritative 'remarks' on language discussed above were contemporary with Boileau's rules for literature and Poussin's for painting. Eighteenth-century Englishmen may not have been prepared to give up as much of their aesthetic freedom as the French, but even they lived in the age of such attempts to regulate expression as Johnson's *Dictionary* (which was normative as well as explanatory), and the foundation of the Royal Academy of Arts, dominated by Johnson's friend, the painter Joshua Reynolds.

The rise of classicism may in turn be viewed as part of a more general rise of self-control or discipline in the West, a major theme in the work of Max Weber, Norbert Elias and Michel Foucault in their studies of capitalism, bureaucracy, table-manners, state formation, schools, prisons and so on, studies which diverge in many respects but agree in identifying an increasing concern in the early modern period with the control of violence, deviance, and even of speech, posture and gesture.[101]

The speed, the extent and the unilinearity of this rise of discipline must not be exaggerated. After all, the eighteenth-century English ideal of conversation appears to have been a little more

[100] Du Refuge (1617), 152.
[101] Burke (1978); Muchembled (1978, 1989); Bremmer and Roodenburg (1991).

relaxed or unbuttoned than that of seventeenth-century France. It was in part a difference in national style. French conversation had the odour of the court, while that of the English still had a whiff of the country. In part, however, the change was part of a more general eighteenth-century reaction against formality, to be observed in many domains, from the repudiation of ritual to the European fashion for informal 'English' gardens.[102]

At the micro level, the changes taking place in the norms of conversation would seem to be related to changing forms of sociability. It can hardly be coincidence that sixteenth-century Italy, seventeenth-century France and eighteenth-century England were all centres of innovation in this respect.

Conversation is often associated (as it was by Guazzo) with privacy, and opposed to oratory or 'public speaking'. Here as elsewhere, however, we should beware of making the distinction between the public and private spheres too sharp, too rigid or too static. 'Why Sir,' as Johnson once remarked, 'it is difficult to say where private conversation begins, and where it ends.'[103]

The frequent references made in the treatises to 'the company' (la brigata, la compagnie, le monde, and so on) make it clear that the 'speech community' of conversation was generally considered to include three or more partners. The kind of occasions the writers of the treatises seem to have had in mind were semi-formal ones, midway between the intimacy of the family and the public stage. Among these occasions were dinner parties (the subject of Guazzo's final chapters) and semi-public assemblies such as 'wakes', academies, salons and clubs.

The term 'wake' is used here without reference to funerals to translate the Italian veglia, an evening visit to the houses of friends. For the patricians of seventeenth-century Genoa, for example, vegliare in conversatione was a winter custom.[104] In the case of Renaissance Italy the most striking example of a new form of sociability was surely the academy, a kind of discussion group for intellectuals which became increasingly common from the later fifteenth century onwards. The 'Platonic Academy' of Marsilio Ficino is a famous example, and so is the group which met in the Rucellai gardens in Florence in the early sixteenth

---

[102]   Burke (1987), 236–7.
[103]   Johnson in Boswell (1934), vol. 4, 216.
[104]   Archivio di Stato, Genoa, fondo Brignole Sale, ms 709.

century and included Niccolò Machiavelli.[105] By the late sixteenth century there were hundreds of academies in Italy and they were becoming increasingly formal institutions with a fixed membership, fixed days for meeting and so on. These groups often discussed the famous *questione della lingua*, and the Florentine Academy (founded in 1542) and the Accademia della Crusca (1582) were particularly concerned with correct forms of language.[106]

From the later sixteenth century onwards, a number of academies or literary circles were founded in France, of which the Académie Française (1634), following the model of the Florentine Academy and the Crusca, was particularly concerned with correct language.[107] These male-dominated groups remained important, but they were supplemented by a French innovation, the salon, which might be defined as a semi-formal social occasion organized by a hostess, normally once a week, for a mixture of ladies and men of letters.

Looking back to Castiglione's *Courtier*, the setting, over which the Duchess of Urbino presided while her sick husband kept to his chember, looks something like a salon, but as far as we know this precedent was not followed in Renaissance Italy, not even by Isabella d'Este at Mantua. In France, on the other hand, such salons can already be found in the sixteenth century, both in the capital and in the provinces.[108]

The golden age of the salon was the seventeenth century, in Paris in particular. The most famous of these groups, especially in the years 1635–48, was that of Cathérine, Marquise de Rambouillet and her daughter Julie, meeting on Saturdays in her house in the Marais, but there were many more, of which the salons of the Marquise de Sablé and the writers Madame de Lafayette and Mademoiselle de Scudéry were particularly well known. Among the writers who frequented these salons were Dominique Bouhours, Jean Chapelain, Vincent Voiture, the Chevalier de Méré, and the Duc de La Rochefoucauld, individuals whose concern with conversation, like that of Madeleine de Scudéry, has already been discussed.[109]

---

[105] Cantimori (1937), 86ff.
[106] Brown (1974); Plaisance (1973); Quondam (1982).
[107] Yates (1947); Boer (1938).
[108] Keating (1941).
[109] Magne (1912); Mongrédien (1947), 20–5, 187; Maclean (1977), 143–54; Dulong (1991).

It seems that language (including conversation itself) was among the favourite topics of conversation in these salons. As in sixteenth-century Italy, the 'language question' was a hot issue in seventeenth-century France, with the place of Florence as a leader of trends or creator of models being taken by the court, especially in the age of Louis XIV.[110] A significant difference between the two, however, was that the French court, unlike 'Florence', was defined as including women, 'Les femmes comme les hommes'.[111] The quality of conversation at the court of Louis XIV must not be exaggerated, however. An Italian observer of the court commented in 1680 that the men spoke of nothing but hunting and horses, the women of clothes.[112] The true theatres in which the theories of polite conversation could be put into practice were the salons.

Given the importance of the salons and their concern with the art of conversation, it is possible that historians of the French language have overestimated the importance of Vaugelas and Bouhours and underestimated the role of women in the development of new standards of polite speech. In this regard it is worth noting that the dialogues of René Bary included female speakers, that the remarks on conversation by the Chevalier de Méré were addressed to a lady, and that the objects of Molière's ridicule were the female supporters of Vaugelas.

At least one male writer of the time complained about female influence on conversation, admitting that it 'polished' men, but claiming that it also 'softened' them ('elle polit les hommes... mais elle les ramollit').[113] One does not have to agree with his judgement to see what he meant. The demand for euphemisms for 'bosom' and even 'face', like the avoidance of the word 'leg' in Victorian England, although formulated by Vaugelas, looks very much like a feminine form of prudery.[114] Again, an important reason for the increasingly strong rejection of the display of learning in conversation was the fact that it excluded all but a few ladies.

Conversation in eighteenth-century England also enjoyed the

---

[110]  Méré (1677), 111; Trotti (1683), 35; Ortigue (1688), 274.
[111]  Vaugelas (1647), preface.
[112]  Visconti (1908), 262.
[113]  Grenaille (1642), 229.
[114]  Vaugelas (1647), 60.

support of new social institutions, such as the coffee-house, the assembly, and the club. The first London coffee-house opened its doors in 1651, and fifty years later there were about five hundred of these places, where the reading of newspapers was combined with discussion or – if we may trust Mr Spectator's reports – with more desultory conversation.

Public assembly-rooms spread in English provincial towns from about 1700 onwards.[115] They were among other things settings for polite conversation between the sexes. The rules of deportment laid down by the famous Master of Ceremonies in the trend-setting Assembly House at Bath, Richard Nash, included a ban on swearing. Addison, however, dismissed conversation in an 'Assembly of Men and Women' because 'the Talk generally runs upon the Weather, Fashions, News and the like publick Topicks.'[116]

Addison may have been articulating a particularly English assumption. Some foreign visitors were surprised at the lack of conversation between ladies and gentlemen in England, and quite amazed at the way in which the sexes were segregated after dinner.[117] Even Swift condemned the habit of making the ladies withdraw after dinner, 'as if it were an established Maxim, that Women are incapable of all Conversation'.[118]

For men, clubs were an increasingly important form of sociability. For literary men there was the Kit Cat Club, which included Congreve, Addison and Steele, and the club Dr Johnson founded in 1764, which met weekly at the Turk's Head in Soho, where Edmund Burke, Oliver Goldsmith, Joshua Reynolds and others 'generally continued their conversation till a pretty late hour'.[119] What we now think of as the traditional London club, in other words an establishment with its own premises, came into existence at this time. Boodle's was founded in 1762, Brook's in 1764, Arthur's 1765. It is tempting to speculate on the possible effects of the clubs on the art of conversation, to ask whether they played a role in replacing the more feminine French model of good conversation with a more masculine one.

[115]   Borsay (1989), 150–62.
[116]   Bond (1965), vol. 1, 289.
[117]   Muralt (1728), 128–9.
[118]   Swift (1939–68), vol. 9, 90.
[119]   Boswell (1934), vol. 1, 477–8.

ORALITY AND PRINT

This essay has necessarily been concerned with precept rather than practice, but the problem of the relation between the two must not be evaded. To argue that everyone followed the precepts all the time is obviously implausible (if they had done so, there would have been no need for the manuals). However, the more limited hypothesis that changes in the system of precepts were followed by similar changes in practice has something to be said for it.

One argument in favour of this hypothesis is the survival of some of these norms until our own time – that of some of us, at least. When I went up to St John's College Oxford in the late 1950s, the conversation of undergraduates at dinner was still subject to rules (which some of us considered archaic) such as 'don't speak more than five words in a foreign language', 'don't talk shop', and 'don't mention a lady's name.' The penalties for rule-breaking were still enforced, at least on occasion, by the practice of 'sconcing', or paying for beer for the challenger's table. The antiquity of the practice – reported at Eton in 1821 as a penalty for quoting Latin – makes it likely that the rules were taken seriously by earlier generations. As for senior combination rooms, I can bear witness that in my own college at Cambridge anyone discovered 'reflecting' upon another fellow is still fined a bottle of claret.

There is also testimony to the influence of printed models on actual speech throughout the early modern period. In the third book of *The Courtier*, Giuliano de' Medici made fun of courtiers who introduce rhetoric or 'inkhorn terms' (*parole di Polifilo*) when speaking to ladies about love. Another reference to the *Hypnerotomachia Poliphili*, a late fifteenth-century Italian romance famous for its Latinate diction, comes from the Venetian patrician Marin Sanudo, who remarked that in his day a certain senator frequently used the phrase *Vocabuli come Pholiphilo* (sic).[120] These references suggest that print had already begun to affect speech in the age of incunabula, and the trend was to continue.

For example, a collection of short stories published in Florence

---

[120]  Castiglione (1528), 3.5, 3.9, 3.70; Sanudo (1980), 205.

in 1572 was entitled 'Book of Stories and of Fine and Noble Speech' (*Libro di novelle e di bel parlar gentile*) as if the dialogues were expected to be consulted by readers who wanted to improve their speaking style. In his instructions to his sons in the 1580s, a Sicilian lawyer, Argisto Giuffredi, advised them to read histories, stories and jest-books because apt stories or witty sayings 'can make a good impression in conversation' ('vi può onorare in una conversatione').[121] It is likely that contemporary readers used Castiglione's *Courtier* for a similar purpose, judging by the frequency with which they marked the jokes, underlining them or sketching a pointing hand in the margin.

A sixteenth-century Spanish treatise on good behaviour went so far as to include a selection of 'commonplaces' of conversation, from gypsies to the Treasury of Venice, while an enterprising Frenchman produced a dictionary of romantic commonplaces in alphabetical order, from *absence* to *yeux*, thus allowing lovers to make a good impression on their mistresses in speech as in writing. These examples illustrate the general thesis that printing encouraged the standardization of speech.[122]

Another means for print to leave its impression on speech habits was through the development, in sixteenth-century Italy, of what were known as 'parlour games', before they were adapted for television. Scipione Bargagli's *Trattenimenti* ('Discussions'), for instance, is a dialogue in which the speakers discuss nine 'honourable and delightful' games, that of 'questions of love' providing a structure for conversations or debates on arms and letters, art and nature, mind and body, and so on. Innocentio Ringhieri's *A Hundred Liberal Games* is even more like an instruction booklet, telling the audience to sit in a circle and choose a leader before discussing whether soldiers are more worthy of love than scholars, and so on.[123]

The influence of print on talk continued throughout the period. Games of *questions* or *maximes d'amour* were played in the salons of Paris. As described by Mlle de Scudéry, they bear a strong resemblance to the games recommended by Ringhieri and Bargagli.[124] Some of the treatises on conversation listed

121  Giuffredi (1896), 84.
122  Palmireno (1577), 33, 66; Des Rues (1603); Eisenstein (1979), 80–8.
123  Bargagli (1587); Ringhieri (1551); Crane (1920), 263–322.
124  Crane (1920), 480–504; Roubert (1972).

below take the form of dialogues and appear to be presented as models for the readers, as Bellegarde's book suggests in its title. A seventeenth-century author drew his readers' attention to anthologies of *bons mots*, while an eighteenth-century guide recommended people wishing to improve their conversation to study 'the Scaligerana . . . and most of those -ana' (in other words collections of the table-talk of famous men), in order to ornament their talk with borrowed phrases.[125] Keeping a commonplace book of material to introduce into conversations was also recommended by some, though others mocked people who collect anecdotes arranged 'in alphabetical order' and lie in wait for opportunities to insert them into a conversation.[126] From the beginning of the eighteenth century onwards, the term 'conversational dictionary' (*Konversationslexikon*) came into use in Germany to describe encyclopaedias, as if one of the main functions of these compilations were to offer a wider range of topics about which to converse.

It is also worth noting that the writers on conversation cited in this essay include novelists, notably Henry Fielding and Mademoiselle de Scudéry (whose romance *Le grand Cyrus* included a transparently disguised description of the Marquise de Rambouillet's salon). Other authors cited above, like Addison and Steele, wrote plays. Their theories of good and bad conversation found expression in their imaginary dialogues. It is therefore worth entertaining the idea that these novels and plays, like the *Polifilo*, affected the speech habits of at least some of their readers, as the dialogues presented on television affect everyday speech habits today, offering them not only ready-made phrases but paradigms of good and bad talk, which may appear no more than 'common sense' but are actually culturally determined norms.

---

[125]  Renaud (1697), 148; Constable (1738), 52.
[126]  Ortigue (1688), 332; Chalesme (1671), 205–6.

*Appendix: a selection of Italian, French and English books
concerned with the art of conversation, 1528 to 1791*

Baldassare Castiglione (1528) *Il Cortegiano*
Alessandro Piccolomini (1543) 'Della conversazione e inter-
tenimento con donne nobili', in *Institutione*, ch. 17
Giovanni Della Casa (1558) *Il Galateo*
Stefano Guazzo (1574) *La civil conversazione*
Anon (1618) *Muximes de bienséance de la conversation*
Jacques du Bosc (1630) *L'honnête femme*
C. Jaunin (1630) *Les compliments*
Claude Favre de Vaugelas (1647) *Remarques sur la langue
française*
R. Bary (1662) *L'esprit de cour*
C. Irson (1662) 'Règles Générales que l'on doit pratiquer dans la
conversation', in his *Nouvelle méthode pour apprendre la
langue française*
Chalesme (1671) 'De la conversation', in his *L'homme de qualité*
Antoine de Courtin (1671) 'Ce qui règle la conversation en
compagnie', in his *Nouvelle traité de la civilité*
Charles Sorel (1672) *De la manière de bien parler*
Dominique Bouhours (1675) *Remarques nouvelles sur la langue
française*
Chevalier de Méré (1677) *Discours de la conversation*
Madeleine de Scudéry (1680) 'De la conversation', and 'De parler
trop ou trop peu', in her *Conversations sur divers sujets*
Joachim Trotti de la Chetardye (1683) *Instructions pour un jeune
seigneur*
Jean La Bruyère (1688) 'De la société et de la conversation', in
*Caractères*
Pierre Ortigue de Vaumorière (1688) *L'art de plaire dans la
conversation*
François de Fenne (1690) 'De la conversation', in *Entretiens
familiers*
François de Callières (1693) *Mots à la mode*
John Locke (1693) *Some Thoughts concerning Education*
Jean-Baptiste de La Salle (1695) *Les règles de la bienséance*
Jean-Bapiste Morvan de Bellegarde (1697) *Modèles de con-
versations pour les personnes polies*

Antoine Renaud (1697) *Manière de parler la langue française selon ses différents styles*
Adam Petrie (1720) *Rules of Good Deportment*
Anne-Thérèse Lambert (1728) *Avis d'une mère*
[J. Constable] (1738) *The Conversation of Gentlemen*
'Simon Wagstaff' [J. Swift] (1738) *Polite Conversation*
Henry Fielding (1743) *Essay on Conversation*
Anon (1757) *Art of Conversation*
J. Swift (1763) 'Hints Towards an Essay on Conversation' (written *c.*1710)
Philip, Lord Chesterfield (1774) *Letters* (written *c.*1748)
J. Trusler (1775) *Principles of Politeness*
J. Boswell (1791) *Life of Johnson*

# 5

## Notes for a Social History of Silence in Early Modern Europe

'Speech consists above all in silence' (Ortega y Gasset)

'We have no history of silence' (George Steiner)

The aim of this essay is to try to sketch the history of the changing meanings of silence in Europe, especially but not exclusively in the early modern period, and at the same time to reflect on the value and the problems of the attempt. The enterprise, in which a few historians have recently engaged, is a complementary opposite of the social history of language, and owes a similar debt to ethnographers of communication.[1] Indeed, this essay was originally inspired by an article by the American anthropologist Keith Basso on silence in Western Apache culture, which argues that the Apache consider it appropriate to keep silent on many occasions when westerners would think it necessary to speak, and more generally that 'a knowledge of when *not* to speak may be as basic to the production of culturally acceptable behavior as a knowledge of what to say.'[2]

To put the point in a more dramatic way, keeping silent is itself an act of communication. As a minor poet of the early nineteenth century, Martin Tupper, put it, 'Well-timed silence

---

[1] Bauman (1983); Nagel and Vecchi (1984); Casagrande and Vecchi (1987); Ciani (1987); Österberg (1991).

[2] Basso (1970), 69. Cf. Tannen and Saville-Troika (1985).

hath more eloquence than speech.' He was echoing a common-place, which had found its way into print in Italy at least in the sixteenth century: 'si dice, ch'un tacere a tempo avanza ogni bel parlare.'[3]

It is the history of this eloquence which will be studied here. The focus will be the deliberate choice not to speak rather than the wider, vaguer topic of the implicit and the unspoken. 'Every act of saying', we are told, 'is a momentary intersection of the said and the unsaid.' The unsaid might be divided into what is taken for granted, the 'silent knowledge' of physical skills which cannot easily be put into words, and taboo topics, like the ones about which Giovanni Della Casa warned his readers (above, p. 101). No attempt will be made here to map these vast territories.[4]

What might be called 'literary' silence, its use by Shakespeare (say) or Harold Pinter, like what the critic George Steiner describes as 'the suicidal rhetoric of silence' in Hölderlin and Rimbaud, will also be excluded from these notes.[5] They will also omit individual choices and focus on what Erving Goffman has called the 'public arrangements' which 'oblige and induce us to be silent', or what another linguist describes as 'institutionally determined' or 'group-determined' silences.[6]

## VARIETIES OF SILENCE

Silence – accompanied by the appropriate gestures or facial expressions – may be warm or cold, intimate or exclusive, polite or aggressive. One medieval writer on ethics, Alain de Lille, described taciturnity as a form of arrogance, George Bernard Shaw called it 'the most perfect expression of scorn', while the British army has or at any rate had a category of offence known as 'dumb insolence'.

This variety of possible meanings explains how one nine-teenth-century manual could claim that 'silence . . . acts a most essential part in a conversation', while another condemned it as 'an ill-bred assumption of superiority'.[7] Again, in seventeenth-

3  Guazzo (1574), 95v.
4  Tyler (1978), 459; Frykman (1990).
5  Steiner (1966); Tannen (1990).
6  Goffman (1981), 121; Saville-Troika (1985).
7  'Sabertash' (1842), 39; Anon (1897), 130.

century France, one famous writer on conversation, the Chevalier de Méré, declared it a 'great fault' to be too fond of keeping silent ('aimer trop à se taire'), while another, the Duc de La Rochefoucauld, wrote of the need 'to know how to be silent' ('savoir se taire').[8]

It is therefore necessary for historians, like linguists and anthropologists, to tune their ears to these varieties.[9] In other words, the meaning of silence varies – like that of other forms of communication, as rhetoricians point out – according to the occasion where silence occurs, according to the person who is silent, and also according to the 'audience', if that is the appropriate word. The moment and the place are also important – the 'locational silence' of temples and libraries, for example.[10] It is necessary to take into account the different uses of silence, its functions, its strategies.

For example, there are many cultures in which it is a rule – or at any rate a male assumption – that women should keep silent, at least in mixed company. In ancient Greece, for example, Aristotle formulated this rule (*Politics*, book 1, 5), supporting his case with a quotation from Sophocles (*Ajax*, line 293), who had in turn quoted a Greek proverb to the effect that 'silence gives grace to woman.' One might describe this proverb as an explicit formulation of the position of women in many cultures, as a 'muted' group which has to structure its world by means of the dominant group's models and vocabulary.[11]

As for the domains or 'regions' of silence, they often include the space around the ruler. At the Byzantine court, there was an official who called for silence when the emperor made his entrance.[12] In similar fashion, there is often a call for silence in court when the judge makes his entrance. A similar space often surrounds the dead, as in the case of the two minutes' silence in contemporary societies.[13] These are all examples of the silence of respect, as La Rochefoucauld called it. So perhaps is the advice given to an American visitor to the Brazilian city of Salvador in

[8] Méré (1677), 112; La Rochefoucauld (1946), 155.
[9] Österberg (1991).
[10] Albertanus (1507), chs 4, 7; Saville-Troika (1985), 16.
[11] Ardener (1975).
[12] Treitinger (1938), 52.
[13] De Vries (1991).

the 1930s: 'Don't talk when you eat with these people...it makes them think you are not enjoying the food.'[14]

Yet another variety is what the sociologist Auguste Comte called a 'conspiracy of silence', for example the *omertà* of Sicily, a reluctance to speak to outsiders about the affairs of the community, especially Mafia business, whether this reluctance is prompted by loyalty or other motives. 'In Italy *omertà* is either fear or complicity' ('In Italia l'omertà si non è paura, è complicità').[15]

An occasion of silence in many societies is a situation of conflict or ambiguity. For example, there is the silence of the man whose response to an insult is not to shout but to plot revenge. 'He says nothing and silence frightens,' as an informant from a culture of the feud, Lebanon, told the anthropologist Michael Gilsenan.[16]

Another anthropologist, Keith Basso, has developed the idea of silence as a form of conflict management. In the article mentioned above, he described the Western Apache as particularly prone to silence in what he called 'social situations in which participants perceive their relationships vis à vis one another to be ambiguous and/or unpredictable'.[17] A recent student of the Icelandic sagas agrees with Basso but develops his ideas further: 'Icelandic men are silent when it is dangerous to speak, and it is almost always dangerous to speak.' She interprets the most frequent types of silence as 'strategies of delay', and notes the importance in the sagas of the idea that 'What is said cannot be taken back.'[18] A sixteenth-century English writer made a similar point when he compared words with money and advised his readers that 'It is pleasure to spend and speak, but hard to call again.'[19]

Even more important is the religious domain. Indeed, it was this aspect of silence which first inspired a scholarly study, a generation before the rise of sociolinguistics; Gustav Mensching's 'Holy Silence' (1926).[20] Silence, it has been suggested, is 'one of

---

14   Landes (1947), 21.
15   Blok (1974), 211–12; poster displayed in Rome, June 1992.
16   Gracián (1646); Gilsenan (1976), 202.
17   Basso (1970), 81; cf. Tannen (1990).
18   Österberg (1991), 19, 26–7.
19   Furnivall (1868a), 89.
20   Mensching (1926).

the essential elements in all religions'.[21] More exactly, we should distinguish varieties of religious silence – personal and communal, pagan and christian, the 'elected silence' of monks, silence in church, and silent or 'mental' prayer. Religious silence is a compound of respect for a deity; a technique for opening the inner ear; and a sense of the inadequacy of words to describe spiritual realities. The philosophical equivalent of this attitude is the famous phrase with which Ludwig Wittgenstein concluded his *Tractatus Logico-Philosophicus*: 'Whereof one cannot speak, thereof must one be silent' ('Wovon man nicht sprechen kann, darüber muss man schweigen').

In classical antiquity, religious silence – 'sacred silence' as Horace called it – is well documented. The silence of Pythagoras and his disciples is particularly well known. Plutarch declared that silence is something 'profound and awesome' and that 'we learn silence from the gods, speech from men.'[22]

The fathers of the church expressed similar views. St Ambrose asked rhetorically, 'What ought we to learn before anything else but to be silent, that we may be able to speak?' When he rewrote Cicero's treatise on duties as a manual of good clerical behaviour, Ambrose included a recommendation of silence as a sign of 'shame' (*maximus actus verecundiae*).[23] St Augustine too had much to say about silent prayer and the eloquence of silence.[24] In the eastern church, silence was associated with asceticism and especially with the ascetics on Mount Athos in the fourteenth century. 'Hesychasm', as their religious silence was called, became a matter of debate, criticized by the western monk Barlaam and defended by Gregory Palamas.

In the medieval West, in Benedictine, Cistercian and especially Carthusian monasteries, silence was the norm, so that an elaborate sign language was to be devised for everyday needs.[25] Where other religious writers emphasized the value of edifying words, monks stressed the spiritual dangers of garrulousness, loquacity and verbosity (*garrulitas, loquacitas, verbositas*).[26]

At a still deeper level, silence changes its meaning as one

21 McCumfrey (1987), 321.
22 Mensching (1926); Ciani (1987); Plutarch (1927–69), vol. 6, 395–467.
23 Ambrose (1984), 97, 128.
24 Mazzeo (1962).
25 Sebeok and Sebeok (1987), 351ff.
26 Gehl (1987).

moves from place to place in the sense that the proportion of speech to silence in a social situation varies greatly between cultures. It was the difference between standard American conventions and those of the Apache which alerted anthropologists such as Dell Hymes and Keith Basso to this problem.

In Europe, too, such differences were and are extremely audible. Many Europeans consider the English to be preternaturally silent, and see 'Mr and Mrs Smith' as they are presented at the beginning of Eugène Ionesco's play *La cantatrice chauve*, which opens with what the stage directions call 'a long moment of English silence'. The English, for their part, regard themselves as normal speakers and the Swedes as preternaturally silent, while the Swedes in turn consider that the truly silent people are the Finns.[27]

## THE SYSTEM OF SILENCE IN
## EARLY MODERN EUROPE

The examples discussed above should help specialists in early modern Europe to incorporate silence into the social history of the period. The first stage with which this section is concerned is to try to see this area and this period as a whole, concentrating on what makes it distinctive from other places and times. The second stage will be to identify changes in the course of the sixteenth, seventeenth and eighteenth centuries. Regional variations will not be ignored, although their systematic analysis will be left for later studies.

The difficulty of finding rich or 'eloquent' sources on this subject may well be imagined. The historian cannot but envy the anthropologists who are able to listen to silence in the field, as Basso did. Excavating the history of speech from written sources produced for other purposes than the historian's is difficult enough, as we have seen, but at least there is a corpus of sources which may be exploited in a reasonably systematic manner. In the case of silence, however, there can be no pretension to being anything more than impressionistic. This essay bears the modest title of 'notes' in recognition of the fact that all a historian can

---

[27]  Lehtonen and Sajavaara (1985).

reasonably hope to do is to extract comment on fragments of information.

Some of these fragments are embedded in judicial records, since disputes generally bring to the surface the implicit expectations of ordinary people in a given culture. Others are to be found in the descriptions of customs by travellers from one part of early modern Europe to another. Here as elsewhere, the wide-ranging curiosity and careful observation of Michel de Montaigne, the seventeenth-century Englishman Philip Skippon, and the eighteenth-century Swiss traveller B. L. de Muralt will be of service.[28]

Further information about the 'rules of silence', as one writer calls them, may be found in the so-called 'conduct-books'.[29] Within this genre there are occasional texts which concentrate on the 'art' of silence, or what one English writer calls 'the government of the tongue'.[30] The Italian moralist Stefano Guazzo noted cases of what he called 'grace in silence' ('grazia nel silenzio'), while the Marquise de Lambert stressed the virtues of a good listener ('il faut savoir bien écouter').[31]

If it were not already clear that the variety of early modern European silences is very great, the point was made clearly and forcibly by two seventeenth-century French writers. La Rochefoucauld distinguished the silence of eloquence, the silence of mockery, and the silence of respect, while Morvan de Bellegarde listed no fewer than eight varieties; prudent, artful, complaisant, mocking, witty, stupid, approving and contemptuous.[32]

All the same, if they are viewed as a whole, the surviving fragments of information do seem to fall into some kind of pattern. To begin with the kinds of people expected to be silent. In the first place, as in the Middle Ages, the monks. Giacomo Affinati, a monk at Padua at the beginning of the seventeenth century, used the form of a dialogue – of all things – to argue that silence is preferable to speech.[33] In Catholic Europe, new monasteries and even new orders were founded. Among the Trappists, a reformed version of the Cistercians, founded in

[28] Cf. Burke (1987), 18–19, 100.
[29] Du Bosc (1632), 19.
[30] Albertanus (1507); Politiano (1547); Allestree (1674); Anon (1682).
[31] Guazzo (1574), 149; Lambert (1843), 105.
[32] La Rochefoucauld (1952); Strosetzki (1978), 23.
[33] Affinati (1606).

seventeenth-century France, the ban on speech was strictest of all, according to the references in their rule to 'a great silence', 'an exact silence', 'a rigorous silence' or 'a perpetual silence', to be broken only in cases of necessity.[34]

In the second place – in order of strictness – women in early modern Europe, as in ancient Greece, were expected to keep quiet. Indeed, in early modern times it was not uncommon to support this rule by quoting Aristotle, or more rarely Democritus.[35] Another favourite authority was St Paul, 'Let the woman learn in silence' (1 *Timothy* 2, 11–12), quoted for example by John Bunyan when he told wives to 'take heed of an idle, talking or brangling tongue' and especially to be silent in the presence of their husbands.[36]

We are of course concerned with degrees of expected silence rather than with absolute prohibitions. As the fourteenth-century Tuscan writer Francesco da Barberino put it, a girl should not keep so silent that people say 'she is dumb', but rather speak or keep silent 'according to the place and the time'.[37] Even in a medieval Mediterranean society, in which females were supposedly subordinate to males, a woman might be praised, at least after her death, because she 'was extremely eloquent and a great talker' ('molto eloquente, grande parlatore'), as in the case of Sandra Morelli, recorded by her descendant Giovanni.[38] Roman courtesans are said to have mocked the ladies of the city for being 'as silent as stones' ('quiete della bocca come sassi'), a comment which reflects some light on their own performances.[39] In eighteenth-century France, the Marquise de Lambert found it necessary to warn her daughter against a proud, insulting silence ('gardez-vous d'avoir un silence fier et insultant').[40]

All the same, silence seems to have been generally regarded as the attribute, or as some Renaissance Italian moralists put it (echoing the Greek proverb quoted above), the 'ornament' of the female sex. 'Silence in a woman always was a sign of gravity and respect; speaking too much was always was a sign of empty-

[34] Anon (1718), 4, 10, 25, 30, 68.
[35] Loredano (1676), 2, 137; León (1583), 60.
[36] Bunyan (1663), 33. Cf. Politiano (1547); León (1583), 41.
[37] Barberino (1957), 12.
[38] Morelli (1956), 184.
[39] Brantôme (1981), 237.
[40] Casagrande and Vecchio (1987), 19; Lambert (1843), 105.

headedness' ('Sempre fu ornamento di gravità e riverenza in una donna la taciturnità: sempre fu costume e indizio di pazzerella il troppo favellare'). Or again, 'Silence is the adornment of women' ('Silentio è ornamento delle donne').[41] A talkative woman might be described as *sfrenata di lingua*, as if men thought she needed a bridle and bit on her tongue – a punishment for scandalmongering literally applied in some places.

It is not difficult to find parallels to this advice in conduct-books from other parts of Europe. The Spanish priest and professor Luis de León declared that the duty of women was 'to stay at home and keep silence' ('las mujeres . . . han de guardar siempre la casa y el silencio').[42] The Frenchman Du Bosc emphasized the need for 'discretion, silence and modesty' in gentlewomen, and advised them to take the Virgin Mary as a model, noting that 'The Holy Scripture makes no mention that ever she spake more than four or five times in all her life.'[43] Similar points are made in English treatises of the early modern period.[44]

Silence was associated with 'shame' or 'modesty' (*vergogne, vergogna*, etc.), the quality which defined respectable women. It may be illustrated by an incident retold in Natalie Davis's well-known book *The Return of Martin Guerre* (though not discussed there from this point of view), in which Bertrande de Rols accepted the intruder Arnaud du Tilh as her true husband by not saying anything when he claimed her. Female silence did indeed have something to do with the notion of sexual honour. A Sicilian lawyer of the sixteenth century reminded his sons that it was safer for wives to speak to strange men only in the presence of their husbands ('Le mogli non ragionano mai co' forestieri più sicuramente che in presenza de' loro mariti').[45]

The rule of silence was applied to certain female groups in particular. Nuns were of course expected to keep particularly quiet, while the Marquise de Lambert advised her readers in early eighteenth-century France that 'Silence is always suitable for a young woman' ('Le silence convient toujours à une jeune personne').[46] Her English equivalents were somewhat more

---

[41]  Alberti (1969), 279; Guazzo (1574), 159r.
[42]  León (1583), 61.
[43]  Du Bosc (1632), 19, 22.
[44]  Bunyan (1663); Savile (1688), 106.
[45]  Giuffredi (1896), 75.
[46]  Cerda (1599), 115–19; Lambert (1843), 105.

liberal. One anonymous author, using the persona of a mother writing to her fifteen-year-old daughter, began by recommending 'a profound silence' in company, 'except when a question is put to you', but went on to allow 'asking some necessary questions, or making some pertinent reflections upon what is said'. Another advised, 'talk little, but never appear speechless and disconcerted, like young creatures just come to town from a Welsh boarding-school.'[47]

Silence was also considered appropriate for children or young people in general. Despite the famous argument of the French historian Philippe Ariès, to the effect that childhood was discovered in seventeenth-century France, plenty of age-related rules of behaviour may be found in other countries and earlier centuries.[48] William Caxton's *Book of Curtesye*, apparently intended for upper-class youths, tells them to be 'hushed in chamber, silent in the hall'.[49] In his well-known conduct-book, Erasmus declared that 'When seated with his elders a boy should never speak unless the occasion demands it or someone invites him to do so . . . Silence is becoming in women but even more so in boys.'[50] An English writer echoed his sentiments later in the sixteenth century: 'Both speech and silence are commendable / But silence is meetest in a child at the table.'[51] Again, an Italian treatise on the court, published early in the seventeenth century, declared that pages (normally aged between seven and fourteen) 'should speak little' ('devono parlar poco').[52] As an eighteenth-century French treatise on conversation put it, 'When one is in the presence of people older than ourselves, or extremely old, it is appropriate to say little . . .' ('Lorsqu'on est avec des personnes qui sont plus âgés que nous, ou fort avancées en âge, il est de la bien séance de parler peu').[53] We are close to the famous Victorian notion that 'children should be seen but not heard.' Indeed, a fifteenth-century text, the *Lytylle Children's Lytil Boke*, did tell its readers: 'Hear and see, and say thou nought.'[54]

[47]   Anon (1775), 79, 86; Anon (1768), 11.
[48]   Nagel and Vecchi (1984).
[49]   Caxton (*c*.1477), line 204.
[50]   Erasmus (1530), 254.
[51]   Seager (1577), 344.
[52]   Timotei (1614), 73.
[53]   Lambert (1843), 168.
[54]   Furnivall (1868b), 20.

Even men might be recommended to keep silent. Like his great predecessor St Ambrose, San Carlo Borromeo, Archbishop of Milan, expected silence and modesty from his clergy. Venetian noblemen in particular seem to have had a reputation for taciturnity. The sixteenth-century Lombard nobleman Sabba Castiglione – to be distinguished from his distant relative Baldassare Castiglione – agreed that it is better to be a man of few words than a *ciarlatore*.[55] *Ciarlare* means 'to chatter', but a *ciarlatore* is reminiscent of a *ciarlatano*, a charlatan, a term used at that time in its literal sense of a man who makes his living by talking on the piazza, telling stories or selling medicines. Castiglione thus associated verbal restraint with nobility and prolixity with salesmen and tradesmen. In England, Ben Jonson echoed the sentiments of Plutarch on the 'disease' of 'talking overmuch'.[56]

Let us turn to the occasions of silence, its 'domains'. It is obvious that monks, women and children were not expected to be silent all the time. Monks sang in choir, women were expected to speak to women, and children to children, or to answer questions from husbands and adults respectively. Conversely, there were occasions of silence for adult males, as in ancient Greece. Greek examples were well known in some circles in early modern Europe. Indeed, Pythagoras on silence is mentioned as often as St Paul. 'Pythagoras wisely kept his disciples in constant silence for two years.'[57] As in Byzantium, courtiers were supposed to be quiet in the prince's presence, out of respect, and not to speak unless they were spoken to. 'Speak rarely in the presence of your lord, unless you are called on' ('Di rado parlate in presenza del Signor vostro, se non ne siete richiesto') was the advice of an Italian treatise on the courtier, echoed by German and French colleagues: 'Let the courtier say little in the presence of the prince' ('Praesente principe pauca loquatur aulicus'); 'His very silence ... will depend on the will of his master ('Son silence même ... dépendra de la volonté de son maître').[58]

Formal meals might be taken in silence, apparently, perhaps

---

[55] Castiglione (1554), no. 42.
[56] Jonson (1953), 27–9.
[57] Timotei (1614), 73. Cf. Guazzo (1574).
[58] Grimaldi quoted Hinz (1992), 234; De Weihe (1615), no. 53 (cf. no. 131); Faret (1630), 49–50.

(as in the Brazilian example quoted above) as a sign of respect for the food and so for the host. We have already seen that children were required to be especially silent at the table. A Czech visitor to England in 1465 observed Elizabeth Woodville, Edward IV's queen, at dinner and noted that 'not a word was spoken', while an Italian visitor around 1500 was surprised by the 'extraordinary silence of everyone' ('un maraviglioso silentio di ciascuno') at a banquet in the City.[59] A description of Elizabethan England, written by a native, noted 'the great silence that is used at the tables of the honourable and wiser sort generally over all the realm'.[60] A contemporary courtesy-book reinforced the message, warning against speaking to the master when he is drinking.[61] Again, in Louis XIV's Versailles, no one spoke to the king during his public meals unless he addressed them first.[62] The surprise of the Italian visitor to London suggests that the custom of eating in silence was not followed there. In a milder version of the rule, however, Stefano Guazzo advised guests not to talk too much, 'because it is said that eloquence is for the piazza and silence for private rooms' ('l'eloquenza è da piazza, e'l silentio da camera').[63]

For his part, the prince often kept silent in front of the courtiers. The kings of Spain from Philip II to Charles II were particularly known for their public taciturnity. Silence may have been their strategy to appear dignified, or it may have been a means of dissimulating their intentions.[64] Even the more outgoing Louis XIV, who took pains to appear accessible, still measured his words in public.[65]

Dissimulation and 'prudent silence' (*prudentemente tacere*) was a central concern of the writers on 'reason of state' and the art of discretion in the early modern period.[66] Appropriately enough, their discussions drew heavily on the writings of Cornelius Tacitus, whose frequent use of the Latin terms for 'silent' suggests his obsession with the subject – appropriate for

[59]  Rozmital (1957), 47; Sneyd (1843), 44.
[60]  Furnivall (1890), 95.
[61]  Furnivall (1868a), 75.
[62]  St-Simon (1983–8), vol. 5, 604.
[63]  Guazzo (1590 edn), 165v.
[64]  Elliott (1987).
[65]  Bluche (1986), 684.
[66]  Pino (1604), 76ff.

someone with his name.[67] A few brief words in Tacitus, such as the phrase 'Tiberius being silent' ('silente Tiberio'), were sometimes sufficient to launch a theorist of reason of state into a long discourse.[68] It is in this context that we should place William the Silent's famous nickname. 'This highly voluble man', as a recent historian has described him, acquired his nickname for his 'deviousness', in other words his ability to dissimulate.[69]

Adult males often kept particularly quiet in the presence of strangers, especially when questioned about the affairs of their community. The conduct associated with *omertà* is not unique to modern Sicily, and is perhaps best understood as an extreme case of a practice traditional in the Mediterranean world. Another special case was that of suspected criminals under interrogation, their silence sometimes assisted by a magical aid, *il maleficio della taciturnità*, a piece of paper bearing words such as the following: 'O holy rope which tied Christ (to the Cross), tie my tongue so that I say nothing, good or bad' ('O santa corda che legasti Cristo / lega la lingua mia / che non dica nè bono nè tristo').[70] The point was that under the system of Roman law, confession was necessary for conviction, so that silence under torture was rewarded by freedom.

Prudence as well as loyalty dictated silence, as a number of proverbs remind us. 'Keep your mouth closed and your eyes open' goes one Italian version, 'Tieni la boccha chiusa e gli occhi aperti.'[71] The Spanish and Portuguese, more vividly, said that a closed mouth keeps out flies ('Em boca cerrada não entra moscas') The Swiss, characteristically perhaps, preferred the commercial metaphor 'Speech is silver, silence is golden' ('Sprechen ist silber, Schweigen ist golden'), a late medieval inscription given wider currency by Carlyle.[72] It is in this tradition that one should place the advice of Shakespeare's Polonius, 'Give every man thy ear, and few thy voice.'

There would seem to be two particularly important principles underlying the system of silence in early modern Europe. In the

---

[67] Gerber (1903), sv 'Silentium', etc.
[68] Forstner (1626), 228.
[69] Swart (1978), 10.
[70] Petrucci (1982), no. 178.
[71] Certaldo (1921), no. 6.
[72] Carlyle (1835), book 3, ch. 3.

first place, within the speech community, the principle of respect, or deference, one of many signs of a fundamentally hierarchical society. Women were supposed to be silent in the presence of men, children in the presence of adults, courtiers in the presence of the prince. The respect of servants for their masters was also supposed to be shown by silence.[73] Silence in church had a similar meaning.

In the second place, especially in relations outside the community, the silence of prudence. This concept should not be understood too narrowly. It was not confined to the silence of fear, but included the dissimulation of princes and the discretion of the wise (described by the Spanish writer Baltasar Gracián in a famous courtesy-book, *El Discreto*).

The problem of the geography of silence has still to be confronted – the problem being that of avoiding two opposite dangers, the failure to notice genuine differences and that of accepting stereotypes too easily, notably the stereotypical contrast between the silent north and the loquacious south. After all, the classical Mediterranean world was able to distinguish between the laconic Lacadaemonians and other more talkative Greeks. Let us look for a moment at two regions, England and Italy.

The observation that the English are unusually taciturn and also tolerant of silence in others was repeated again and again in the early modern period, by natives and foreigners alike. Thus Addison noted in *The Spectator* (1711) that 'The English delight in Silence more than any other European Nation, if the Remarks which are made on us by Foreigners are true'. and admitted that 'Our Discourse is not kept up in Conversation, but falls into more Pauses and Intervals than in our Neighbouring Countries.'[74] Even Dr Johnson was described by a friend as 'like the ghosts, who never speak till they are spoken to'.[75]

One of the most memorable foreign accounts of the peculiarities of the English in this respect comes from the pen of a Swiss traveller, Muralt. Muralt compares the taciturnity of the English with that of their dogs, and describes gentlemen after dinner as quietly smoking their pipes after the ladies have left, breaking the silence every now and then to ask 'How d'ye do?' His description

73   Sagittarius (1603), 616.
74   Bond (1965), vol. 2, 32; cf. Constable (1738), 90.
75   Piozzi (1974), 130.

may well seem too amusing to be true, but it is followed by a careful and sympathetic analysis of the place of silence in English culture, reminiscent of Basso on the Western Apache. For example, Muralt contrasts the French tendency to speak when there is nothing to say, with the English preference for 'communicating feelings rather than words'. He also notes the lack of a mean between 'complete familiarity and respectful silence'.[76] In other words, English silence was not universal, but varied with the company.

The idea of the talkative southerner is also in need of qualification. For example, the reserved silence of the Spaniards often drew comments of surprise from foreigners, who sometimes compared both kings and viceroys to statues. Travelling in Lombardy, Addison perceived a contrast between the 'talkative' French and the 'reserved' Italians.[77]

Again, Italian sources contain a good many warnings of the dangers of talking. Thus Paolo da Certaldo declared that one should 'be silent ten times and speak once' because 'you will repent speaking far more often than keeping quiet', and went on to recommend his readers not to reveal their secrets to anyone without being certain that he is trustworthy ('i tuoi segreti non manifestare a persona che tu non sia ben cierto di lui').[78] In similar fashion, Giovanni Morelli told his sons to 'keep quiet' ('statti cheto') and especially 'not to criticize or speak ill of people in the government, or their business' ('guarti di non biasimare ne' dire male di loro imprese e faccende').[79]

Such recommendations may perhaps be explained in terms of a culture of distrust which some scholars consider to be particularly Italian or at least Mediterranean.[80] In any case, the existence of this tradition of advice strikes a powerful blow to the stereotype of the loquacious southerner.

It may be objected that precepts of this kind are poor evidence of practice, since there would be no need to recommend a certain style of behaviour if people were already following the rules. The objection is a weighty one, but a possible answer to it has already

[76]   Muralt (1728), 126, 128, 130–1
[77]   Addison (1705), 373.
[78]   Certaldo (1921), nos 74, 97.
[79]   Morelli (1956), 275.
[80]   Weissman (1985).

been offered (above, p. 95), to the effect that changes in precept are likely to be sensitive indicators of changes in practice. It is time to offer a few suggestions about changes over the sixteenth, seventeenth and eighteenth centuries.

## CHANGES IN THE SYSTEM, 1500 TO 1800

The fragmentary evidence available does not allow confident generalizations about trends over the long term, but it is at least possible to offer a few provisional hypotheses about change in three domains: the religious, the political and the domestic.

In the first place, the Reformations, Catholic and Protestant, had their effect on speech and silence as on so many aspects of everyday life. When the abbeys were suppressed in northern Europe at the Reformation, the ideal of monastic silence was slow to disappear. One does not normally think of Martin Luther as a silent man, but it seems that the habits of the cloister were not easy to break. He did not always talk at table, but according to one witness, Johannes Mathesius, he 'sometimes kept silence for the whole meal in the manner of his old monastery' ('bissweylen die gantze malzeyt sein alt Kloster silentium hielt').[81]

However, the Reformation brought changes too. A sixteenth-century dialogue, the Cymbalum Mundi, has been interpreted as a defence of hesychasm in a new context, that of the religious disputes of the Reformation.[82] Another form of religious silence which was increasingly important in the age of religious wars was 'Nicodemism', in other words dissimulation of one's true opinions, so called after Nicodemus, who came to Christ by night.[83] The most spectacular change of all, however, was surely the attempt to extend the eloquence of silence from the cloister into the church.

On the Catholic side, we see a general attempt to draw sharper boundaries between the sacred and the profane which included attempts to make the faithful behave more respectfully in church. The Council of Trent concerned itself with the problem. So did

[81]   Stolt (1964), 15.
[82]   Nurse (1968).
[83]   Cantimori (1939), 70; Ginzburg (1970).

Pope Pius V, who issued a special decree against walking, talking and laughing during Mass. A leading canon lawyer, Martín de Azpilcueta, devoted a whole treatise to the subject of ecclesiastical silence.[84] San Carlo Borromeo, Archbishop of Milan, penalized talking in church with up to ten days on bread and water. In similar fashion, the bishop of Tortona issued an edict in 1576 against talking in church, especially concerning secular business or 'profane' matters ('cose profane, negotii secolari').[85] How far these rules were effective it is of course difficult to say. A contemporary observer of Italians in church may be permitted to be at least a little sceptical of their efficacy. It is interesting to discover that as early as 1580 a foreign observer with a keen ehtnographic eye, Michel de Montaigne, passing through Verona, was surprised to discover that the men 'were talking in the very choir of the church' during Mass, with their backs to the altar ('ils devisaient au choeur même de l'église').[86]

References in sermons and elsewhere suggest a similar concern for silence in Protestant churches. 'Paul's Walk', an aisle inside Old St Paul's, was a traditional meeting-place for merchants and others, but seventeenth-century preachers such as John Angier denounced 'walking and talking in the church' and whispering 'in time of prayer' as marks of disrespect for God.[87] A still more dramatic contrast with Catholic practice was the positive attitude to silence on the part of the Quakers, who regarded words as a sign of wilfulness and as part of the corrupt outer world. It was for this reason that William Dewsbury, for example, warned his brethren, 'Take heed of many words.' The most striking illustration of the Quakers' rejection of speech was the institution of the 'silent meeting', a form of worship without set words and sometimes without words at all.[88]

The rise of absolute monarchy seems to have been accompanied by a rise of silence in the political domain. The increasing numbers of spies in government service made it more dangerous to speak about politics in public, while speech like other forms of

[84] Azpilcueta (1582).
[85] Tacchella (1966), 75–6.
[86] Montaigne (1992), 64.
[87] Angier (1647), 74; cf. Furnivall (1868a), 74, 346.
[88] Bauman (1983), 21–3, 121–8.

behaviour at court was subject to increasingly strict control, best documented at the model courts of Madrid and Versailles. Like the soldier, the courtier was increasingly expected to demonstrate self-control or discipline, or to use the language of the time, *continentia* and *coerctio*. The rituals of Versailles, like the formal dances which noblemen and noblewomen learned at this time, may be seen as a means to this end. The manuals of conversation, discussed in an earlier chapter, which instructed their readers when to speak and when to be silent, at court and elsewhere, played their part in this development.[89]

The large number of manuals of conversation in circulation in early modern Europe suggest an increasing concern with self-control in the private or domestic sphere, in other words the rise of what Norbert Elias used to call 'civilization', and Michel Foucault, 'discipline' (above, p. 113). The manuals of table manners, with their stress on silence during meals, point in the same direction.

In other words, the 'government of the tongue', as one English writer, Richard Allestree, called it, was related to some of the major cultural and social trends in early modern Europe; the Renaissance, the Reformation, and the rise of absolute monarchy. Given the comparison, made by a sixteenth-century Englishman, between spending and saving words and money, it is also tempting to speculate about a possible relation between the rise of silence (or more precisely, controlled speech) and the rise of capitalism.

It is even more tempting to speculate about the possibility that in the realm of silence as in other spheres (from gesture to sexual honour or attitudes to hygiene), the attitudes and behaviour of northern and southern Europeans gradually diverged in the course of the sixteenth and seventeenth centuries. The divergence might be illustrated by the complaint of an English visitor to a playhouse in Venice, that the audience 'stamp'd and whistled and call'd to one another', while 'Some of the noblemen that stood near the stage would often interrupt the actors and discourse with them.'[90] The rise of bodily self-control, including the 'bridling of the tongue', was a general European movement, but it seems to have been more effective or more rapidly effective in the Protestant than in the Catholic world, thus widening the gap between the

---

[89] Foucault (1975); Oestreich (1982), esp. 52–4.
[90] Skippon (1732), 502.

more silent, self-controlled, individualistic, democratic, capitalist, cold north, and the more talkative, spontaneous, disorderly, familistic, feudal, warm south. But enough of speculation. The rest, as Hamlet said, is silence.

# Bibliography

Secondary works are cited in English translation wherever possible, primary sources in the original language. The names in square brackets are those of the presumed authors of anonymous works.

H. Aarsleff (1967) *The Study of Language in England 1780–1860*, Princeton

P. Adami (1946) *Regole che s'osservano nelle scuole de' padri della Compagnia di Giesù nel loro collegio di Santa Lucia in Bologna*, ed. N. Fabrini, Rome

J. Addison (1705) *Remarks on Several Parts of Italy*; rpr. London 1890

G. Affinati (1606) *Il muto che parla*, Venice.

E. A. Ahern (1981) *Chinese Ritual and Politics*, Cambridge

N. Ahnlund (1943) 'Diplomatiens språk i Sverige', in Ahnlund, *Svenskt och Nordiskt*, Stockholm, 114–22

J. Aitchison (1981) *Language Change: Progress or Decay?*, London

Albertanus (1507) *De loquendi ac tacendi modo*, Paris; vernacular version in his *Trattati morali*, ed. F. Selmi, Bologna 1873, 1–40

L. B. Alberti (1969) *I libri della famiglia*, ed. R. Romano and A. Tenenti, Turin

B. Aldrete (1606) *Del origen y principio de la lengua castellana*, Rome

[R. Allestree] (1673) *The Lady's Calling*, Oxford

[R. Allestree] (1674) *The Government of the Tongue*, Oxford

L. Althusser (1970) 'Ideology and Ideological State Apparatuses', English trans. in Althusser, *Lenin and Philosophy*, London 1971, 121–73

Ambrose (1984) *De officiis ministrorum*, ed. M. Testard, Paris

R. Andersen (1988) *The Power and the Word: Language, Power and Change*, London

B. Anderson (1983) *Imagined Communities: Reflections on the Origin and Spread of Nationalism*; 2nd edn., London 1991

J. Angier (1647) *An Help to Better Hearts*, London

Anon (1618) *Maximes de la bienséance en la conversation/Maximes de la gentillesse et de l'honnesteté en la conversation*; new edn Paris 1663

Anon (1677) *The Art of Complaisance, or the Means to Oblige in Conversation*, 2nd edn, London

Anon (1682) 'L'Art de se taire', *Mercure Galant*, February

Anon (1719) *Reglemens de l'abbaye de Notre-Dame de la Trappe*, Paris

Anon (1757) *The Art of Conversation*, London

Anon (1768) *The Lady's Preceptor*, Birmingham

Anon (1775) *The Polite Lady*, London

Anon (1897) *The Art of Conversation*, New York

G. Antoniazzi, ed. (1957) *Rerum Novarum*, Rome

G. Aquilecchia (1967) 'Pietro Aretino e la lingua zerga'; rpr. in Aquilecchia, *Schede di italianistica*, Turin 1976, 153–69

G. Aquilecchia (1976) 'U e non-U nell'italiano Parlato', in Aquilecchia, *Schede di italianistica*, Turin, 313–30

S. Ardener (1975) 'Introduction', to *Perceiving Women*, ed. Ardener, London, vii–xxii

S. Arditi (1970) *Diario*, ed. R. Cantagalli, Florence

P. Aretino (1975) *Sei giornate*, ed. P. Aquilecchia, Bari

C. Armstrong (1965) 'The Language Question in the Low Countries', in *Europe in the Late Middle Ages*, ed. J. R. Hale, R. Highfield and B. Smalley, London

E. Armstrong (1954) *Robert Estienne, Royal Printer*, Cambridge

J. Armstrong (1982) *Nations before Nationalism*, Chapel Hill

A. R. Ascoli (1987) *Ariosto's Bitter Harmony*, Princeton

M. Atkinson (1984) *Our Masters' Voices*, London

R. Auernheimer (1973) *Gemeinschaft und Gespräch*, Munich

F. C. B. Avé-Lallemant (1858–62) *Das deutsche Gaunerthum*, 4 vols, Leipzig

M. de Azpilcueta (1582) *El silencio ser necessario en el choro*, Rome

C. Backvis (1958) *Quelques remarques sur le bilinguisme latino-polonais dans la Pologne du* xvie *siècle*, Brussels

M. L. Baeumer (1984) 'Luther and the Rise of the German Literary Language: a Critical Reassessment', in Scaglione (1984b), 95–117

M. M. Bakhtin (under the name V. S. Voloshinov) (1929) *Marxism and the Philosophy of Language*, English trans. New York 1973

M. M. Bakhtin (1940) 'Discourse in the Novel', English trans. in Bakhtin, *Dialogic Imagination*, Austin 1981, 259–422

M. M. Bakhtin (1952–3) 'The Problem of Speech Genres', English trans. in Bakhtin, *Speech Genres and Other Late Essays*, ed. C. Emerson and M. Holquist, Austin 1986, 60–102

M. M. Bakhtin (1965) *Rabelais and his World*, English trans. Cambridge Mass. 1968

B. Balbín (1775) *Dissertatio apologetica*, Prague

A. Balcells, ed. (1980) *Història dels Països Catalans*, Barcelona

D. Baltzell (1958) *Philadelphia Gentlemen*, New York

M. Barbagli (1984) *Sotto lo stesso tetto*, Bologna

C. Barber (1976) *Early Modern English*, London

F. da Barberino (1957) *Reggimento e costumi della donna*, ed. G. E. Sansone, Turin

S. Bargagli (1587) *Trattenimenti*, Venice

H. Baron (1955) *The Crisis of the Early Italian Renaissance*, Princeton

R. Bary (1662) *L'esprit de cour, ou les conversations galantes*, Paris

B. Basile (1984) 'Uso e diffusione del latino', in Formigari, 333–46

K. H. Basso (1970) 'To Give up on Words: Silence in Western Apache Culture', rpr. in Giglioli (1972), 67–86

K. H. Basso (1974) 'The Ethnography of Writing', in Bauman and Sherzer, 425–32

F. de Bassompierre (1665) *Mémoires*, Cologne

M. Batllori (1983) 'El català, llengua de cort a Roma durant els pontificats de Calixt III i Alexandre VI', *Actes del Sisè Col.loqui Internacional de Llengua i Literatura Catalanes*, ed. G. Tavani and J. Pinell, Montserrat, 509–21

R. Bauman (1983) *Let Your Words be Few*, Cambridge

R. Bauman and J. Sherzer, eds (1974) *Explorations in the Ethnography of Speaking*, Cambridge

G. L. Beccaria (1968) *Spagnolo e Spagnoli in Italia*, Turin

G. L. Beccaria, ed. (1973) *I linguaggi settoriali in Italia*, Milan

M. Becker (1971) 'An Essay on the Quest for Identity in the Early Italian Renaissance', in *Florilegium Historiale*, ed. J. G. Rowe and W. H. Stockdale, Toronto, 295–312

M. van Beek (1969) *An Enquiry into Puritan Vocabulary*, Groningen

O. Behaghel (1898) *Geschichte der deutsche Sprache*, Berlin and Leipzig

H. Belloc (1902) *The Path to Rome*, London

P. Bembo (1525) *Prose della volgar lingua*, Venice

J. Benedicti (1602) *Somme des pechez*, Paris

T. Bennett et al., eds (1981) *Culture, Ideology and Social Process*, London

J. Béranger (1969) 'Latin et langues vernaculaires dans la Hongrie du 17e siècle', *Revue Historique* 242, 5–28

G. Bergmann (1988) *Gedenkschriften*, Antwerp

B. Bernstein (1971) *Class, Codes and Control*, London

S. Bertelli (1976) 'L'egemonia linguistica come egemonia culturale', *Bibliothèque d'humanisme et renaissance* 38, 249–81

B. Beugnot (1979) 'Débats autour du Latin dans la France classique', *Acta Conventus Neo-Latini Amstelodamensis*, ed. P. Tuynman et al., Munich, 93–106

T. Beza (1554) *Epistola Magistri Benedicti Passavantii*, ed. I. Lisieux, Paris 1875

J. W. Binns (1990) *Intellectual Culture in Elizabethan and Jacobean England: the Latin Writings of the Age*, Leeds

J. Birch, ed. (1742) *Thurloe Papers*, 7 vols, London

V. da Bisticci (1970–6) *Vite*, ed. A. Greco, 2 vols, Florence

E. Blackall (1959) *The Emergence of German as a Literary Language*, Cambridge

M. Bloch (1939–40) *Feudal Society*, English trans. London 1961

M. Bloch, ed. (1975) *Political Language and Oratory in Traditional Societies*, New York

A. Blok (1974) *The Mafia in a Sicilian Village*, Oxford

F. Bluche (1986) *Louis XIV*, English trans. London 1990

T. Boccalini (1678) *La Bilancia Politica*, 3 vols, Châtelaine

S. Bochart (1692) *Opera*, Leiden

J. de Boer (1938) 'Men's Literary Circles in Paris, 1610–60', *Papers of the Modern Language Association* 53, 730–80

D. F. Bond, ed. (1965) *The Spectator*, 5 vols, Oxford

V. Borghini (1971) *Scritti inediti o rari sulla lingua*, ed. J. R. Woodhouse, Bologna

G. Borrow (1843) *The Bible in Spain*, ed. U. R. Burke, 2 vols, London

P. Borsay (1989) *The English Urban Renaissance*, Oxford

A. Borst (1957–63) *Der Turmbau von Babel*, 4 vols, Stuttgart

J. du Bosc (1632) *L'honnête femme*, Paris

J. Bossy (1975) *The English Catholic Community*, London

J. Boswell (1934) *Life of Johnson*, ed. G. B. Hill, rev. edn., 6 vols, Oxford

P. Bourdieu (1972) *Outlines of a Theory of Practice*, English trans. Cambridge 1977

P. Bourdieu (1979) *Distinction*, English trans. London 1984

P. Bourdieu (1991) *Language and Symbolic Power*, Cambridge

H. Boyer and P. Gardy, eds (1985) *La question linguistique au sud au moment de la Révolution française*, Montpellier (special issue 17 of *Lengas*)

L. van den Branden (1956) *Het streven naar verheerlijking van het Nederlands in de 16de eeuw*, Arnhem

C. M. B. Brann, ed. (1991) *Rise and Development of National European Languages*, special issue 1/2 of *History of European Ideas* 13

P. de Brantôme (1981) *Les dames galantes*, ed. P. Pia, Paris

F. Braudel (1979) *The Wheels of Commerce*, English trans. London 1982

J. Bremmer and H. Roodenburg, eds (1991) *A Cultural History of Gesture*, Cambridge

D. R. Brenneis and F. L. Myers, eds (1984) *Dangerous Words*, London and New York

J. Breuilly (1982) *Nationalism and the State*, Manchester

A. Briggs (1960) 'The Language of Class in Early Nineteenth Century England', rpr. in Briggs, *Collected Essays*, Brighton 1985, vol. 1, 3–33

L. F. Brosnahan (1963) 'Some Historical Cases of Language Imposition', in *Language in Africa*, ed. J. Spencer, Cambridge, 7–24

P. Brown and S. Levinson (1987) *Politeness*, Cambridge

P. M. Brown (1974) *Lionardo Salviati*, Oxford

R. Brown and A. Gilman (1960) 'The Pronouns of Power and Solidarity'; rpr. in Giglioli (1972), 252–80

R. Brown and A. Gilman (1989) 'Politeness Theory and Shakespeare's Four Major Tragedies', *Language in Society* 18, 159–212

E. Browne (1673) *A Brief Account of Some Travels*; rpr. Munich 1975

E. Browne (1923) *Journal*, ed. G. Keynes, Cambridge

A. Brun (1923) *Recherches historiques sur l'introduction du français dans les provinces du Midi*, Paris

J. Brunet (1976) 'Le paysan et son langage dans l'oeuvre théatrale de Giovanmaria Cecchi', in *Ville et campagne dans la littérature italienne de la Renaissance*, ed. A. Rochon, Paris, 179–266

J. Brunet (1978) 'Un "langage colakeutiquement profane", ou l'influence de l'Espagne sur la troisième personne de politesse italienne', in *Presence et influence de l'Espagne dans la culture italienne de la Renaissance*, ed. A. Rochon, Paris, 251–315

O. Brunner, W. Conze and R. Koselleck, eds (1972–90, in progress) *Geschichtliche Grundbegriffe*, 6 vols, Stuttgart

J. Bunyan (1663) *Christian Behaviour*; ed. J. S. McGee, Oxford 1987

F. Brunot (1905–53) *Histoire de la langue française*, 13 vols, Paris

A. Buck (1978) 'Dante und die Ausbildung des italienische Nationalbewusstseins', in *Nationen*, vol. 1, ed. H. Beumann and W. Schröder, Sigmaringen, 489–503

R. Buckle, ed. (1978) *U and Non-U Revisited*, London

J. Burckhardt (1860) *Civilisation of the Renaissance in Italy*, English trans. rpr. Harmondsworth 1991

P. Burke (1978) *Popular Culture in Early Modern Europe*, London

P. Burke (1987) *Historical Anthropology of Early Modern Italy*, Cambridge

P. Burke (1989) 'History as Social Memory', in *Memory*, ed. T. Butler, Oxford, 97–113

P. Burke (*c*.1993a) 'Translations into Latin in Early Modern Europe', forthcoming in *Il Latino nell'età moderna*, ed. R. Avesani, Bologna

P. Burke (*c*.1993b) 'Cities, Spaces and Rituals in the Early Modern World', forthcoming in *Ritual Spaces in Holland and Italy*, ed. H. de Mare and A. Vos, Assen

P. Burke and R. Porter, eds (1987) *The Social History of Language*, Cambridge

P. Burke and R. Porter, eds (1991) *Language, Self and Society*, Cambridge

G. Burnet (1686), *Some Letters*, Amsterdam

T. Bynon (1977) *Historical Linguistics*, Cambridge

F. de Callières (1693) *Mots à la mode*, Paris

J.-L. Calvet (1974) *Linguistique et colonialisme*, Paris

J.-L. Calvet (1987) *La guerre des langues*, Paris

J. Calvin (1863–1900) *Opera*, ed. G. Baum, E. Cunitz and C. Reuss, Berlin and Brunswick

D. Cameron, ed. (1990) *The Feminist Critique of Language*, London

P. Camporesi, ed. (1973) *Il libro dei vagabondi*, Turin

D. Cantimori (1937) 'Rhetoric and Politics in Italian Humanism', *Journal of the Warburg Institute* 1, 83–102

D. Cantimori (1939) *Eretici italiani del '500*, Florence

G. C. Capaccio (1882) 'Descrizione di Napoli', *Archivio Storico per le Provincie Napoletane* 7, 68–103, 531–54, 776–97

Andreas Capellanus (1941) *De amore*, ed. and trans. J. J. Parry, New York

D. Carafa (1971) *Dello optimo cortesano*, ed. G. Paparelli, Salerno

Thomas Carlyle (1835) *Sartor Resartus*; new edn. London 1880

M. Carneiro da Cunha (1986) *Negros, estrangeiros*, São Paulo

C. Casagrande and S. Vecchi (1987) *I Peccati della lingua: disciplina e etica della parola nella cultura medievale*, Rome

B. Castiglione (1528) *Il Cortegiano*, ed. B. Maier, Turin

S. Castiglione (1554) *Ricordi*, Venice

A. Castro (1941) *La peculiaridad lingüística rioplatense y su sentido histórico*, Buenos Aires

W. Caxton (*c*.1477) *Book of Courtesy*, London

A. Debà (1617) *Il cittadino de repubblica*, Genoa

J. de la Cerda (1599) *Vida política de mujeres*, Alcalà

P. da Certaldo (1921) *Il libro di buoni costumi*, ed. S. Morpurgo, Florence

M. de Certeau, J. Revel and D. Julia (1975) *Une politique de la langue*, Paris

S. Cerutti (1988) 'Du corps au métier', *Annales E.S.C.* 43, 323–52

S. Cerutti (1992) *Mestieri e privilegi*, Turin

F. Chabod (1961) *L'idea di nazione*, ed. A. Saitta and E. Sestan, Bari

Chalesme (1671) *L'homme de qualité*, Paris

D. Chambers (1970) *The Imperial Age of Venice*, London

F. Charpentier (1676) *Défense de la langue française*, Paris

A. Chastel (1954) 'Un épisode de la symbolique urbaine au xve siècle: Florence et Rome, cités de Dieu', in *Urbanisme et architecture*, Paris

G. Chastellain (1863) *Chronique*, ed. L. de Lettenhove, Brussels

Chazet (1812) *L'art de causer*, Paris

Chesterfield, Lord (1774) *Letters*; rpr. London 1929

F. Chiappelli (1969) *Nuovi studi sul linguaggio del Machiavelli*, Florence

F. Chiappelli, ed. (1985) *The Fairest Flower: the Emergence of Linguistic National Consciousness in Renaissance Europe*, Florence

T. Childen (1990) 'The Social Language of Politics in Germany', *American Historical Review* 95, 331–58

M. G. Ciani (1987) *The Regions of Silence*, Amsterdam

M. T. Cicero (1913) *De officiis*, ed. W. Miller, Cambridge, Mass.

A. Cicourel (1973) *Cognitive Sociology*, Harmondsworth

L. Cimber and F. Danjou, eds (1836) *Archives curieuses, première série*, Paris

C. Cittadini (1604) *Le origini della volgar toscana favella*, Siena

Clarendon, Lord (1888) *History*, ed. W. D. Macray, 6 vols, Oxford

K. Clark and M. Holquist (1984) *Bakhtin*, Cambridge, Mass.

J. Cleland (1607) *Heropaideia, or the Institution of a Young Nobleman*, London

K. Cmiel (1990) *Democratic Eloquence: the Fight over Popular Speech in Nineteenth-Century America*, Berkeley

W. Coates (1969) 'The German Pidgin-Italian of the Sixteenth-Century Lanzichenecchi', Papers from the 4th Annual Kansas Linguistics Conference, 66–74

A. P. Cohen, ed. (1982) *Belonging*, London

B. Cohn (1985) 'The Command of Language and the Language of Command', *Subaltern Studies* 4, ed. R. Guha, Delhi, 276–329

V. Coletti (1983) 'Il volgare al Concilio di Trento', in Coletti, *Parole dal pulpito: chiesa e movimenti religiosi tra latino e volgare*, Casale, 189–211

[J. Constable] (1738) *The Conversation of Gentlemen*, London

E. Conte (1985) *Accademie studentesche a Roma nel '500*, Rome

R. L. Cooper, ed. (1982) *Language Spread*, Bloomington

P. J. Corfield (1991) 'Historians and Language', in *Language, History and Class*, ed. Corfield, Oxford, 1–29

C. Corrain and P. L. Zampini, eds (1970) *Documenti etnografici e folkloristici nei sinodi diocesani italiani*, Bologna

M. Cortelazzo (1983) 'Uso, vitalità e espansione del dialetto', in *Storia della cultura veneta*, vol. 4, part 1, Padua, 363–79

B. Cottle (1969) *The Triumph of English 1350–1400*, London

G. Coulton (1940) *Europe's Apprenticeship*, London

G. Courthop (1907) *Memoirs*, ed. S. C. Lomas, London

A. de Courtin (1671) *Nouvelle traité de la civilité*, Paris

G. Cozzi, ed. (1980) *Stato, società e giustizia nella repubblica veneta*, Rome

G. Craig (1982) *The Germans* (appendix, 'The Awful German Language'), Harmondsworth

T. F. Crane (1920) *Italian Social Customs of the Sixteenth Century*, New Haven

J. Cremona (1965) 'Dante's Views on Language', in *The Mind of Dante*, ed. U. Limentani, Cambridge, 138–62

B. Croce (1917) *La Spagna nella vita italiana durante la Rinascenza*, Bari

T. Crowley (1989) *The Politics of Discourse: the Standard Language Question in British Cultural Debates*, London

J. Culler (1976) *Saussure*, London

A. Dardi (1984) 'Uso e diffusione del francese', in Formigari, 347–72

M. Dascal (1992) 'On the Pragmatic Structure of Conversation', in Parret and Verschueren, 35–56

N. Davies (1984) *Heart of Europe*, Oxford

N. Z. Davis (1983) *The Return of Martin Guerre*, Cambridge, Mass.

M. Dazzi, ed. (1956) *Il fiore della lirica veneziana*, 4 vols, Venice

J.-P. Dedieu (1979) 'Les disciplines du langage et du société', in *L'Inquisition espagnole*, ed. B. Bennassar et al., Paris, 244–67

J. V. Delacroix (1770–1) 'Lettre d'un grand amateur de la langue latine', *Spectateur Français, 11e discours*, Paris

G. Della Casa (1558) *Il Galateo*, ed. D. Provenzal, Milan 1950

A. Denis (1979) *Charles VIII et les italiens*, Geneva

J.-P. Dens (1973) 'L'art de la conversation au 17e siècle', *Les Lettres Romanes* 27, 215–24

J. Derrida (1972) 'Plato's pharmacy', in Derrida, *Dissemination*, English trans. Chicago 1981, ch. 1

E. Deschanel (1857) *Histoire anecdotique de la conversation*, Leipzig

G. Devoto (1972) *Scritti minori*, vol. 3, Florence

Dio Chrysostom (1939–51) *Discourses*, 5 vols, Cambridge, Mass

S. K. Donaldson (1979) 'One Kind of Speech Act: How Do We Know When We're Conversing?', *Semiotica* 28, 259–99

M. Douglas (1966) *Purity and Danger*, London

G. W. J. Drewes (1929) 'The Influence of Western Civilization on the Language of the East Indian Archipelago', in *The Effect of Western Influence on Native Civilizations in the Malay Archipelago*, ed. B. Schrieke, Batavia, 126–57

Dufferin, Marquis of (1903) *Letters from High Latitudes*, 11th edn, London

C. Dulong (1991) 'De la conversation à la création', in *Histoire des femmes en occident*, vol. 3, ed. N. Z. Davis and A. Farge, Paris, 403–25

A. Dundes, L. Leach and B. Özkök (1972) 'The Strategy of Turkish Boys' Verbal Duelling Rhymes', in Gumperz and Hymes, 130–60

M. Durante (1981) *Dal Latino all'italiano moderno*, Bologna

V. Durkacz (1983) *The Decline of the Celtic Languages*, Edinburgh

J. Edwards (1985) *Language, Society and Identity*, London

E. Eisenstein (1979) *The Printing Press as an Agent of Change*, 2 vols, Cambridge

N. Elias (1939) *The Civilizing Process*, English trans. in 2 vols Oxford 1981–2

J. Elliott (1987) 'The Court of the Spanish Habsburgs'; rpr. in Elliott, *Spain and its World 1500–1700*, New Haven 1989

Erasmus (1530) *De civilitate morum puerilium*, Paris

H. Estienne (1578) *Deux dialogues du nouveau langage français*, ed. P. M. Smith, Geneva, 1980

R. J. W. Evans (1979) *The Making of the Habsburg Monarchy*, Oxford

J. Evelyn (1955) *Diary*, ed. E. S. De Beer, 6 vols, Oxford

B. Fabian (1985) 'Englisch als neue Fremdsprache des 18. Jhts', in Kimpel, 178–96

J. Fabian (1986) *Language and Colonial Power*, Cambridge

N. Fairclough (1989) *Language and Power*, Harmondsworth

N. Faret (1630) *L'honnête homme ou l'art de plaire à la cour*, ed. M. Magendie, Paris 1925

L. Febvre (1942) *The Problem of Unbelief in the Sixteenth Century*, English trans. Cambridge, Mass. 1982

B. Feijoó y Montenegro (1781) *Teatro Critico Universal*, 8 vols, Madrid

J. Fentress and C. Wickham (1992) *Social Memory*, London

M. Feo (1986) 'Tradizione latina', in *Letteratura italiana*, ed. A. Asor Rosa, vol. 5, Turin, 311–78

C. A. Ferguson (1959) 'Diglossia'; rpr. in Giglioli (1972), ch. 11

H. Fielding (1743) *Essay on Conversation*, London

Piero Fiorelli (1984) 'La lingua giuridica dal De Luca al Buonaparte', in Formigari, 127–56

L. Firpo, ed. (1985) *Il supplizio di Tommaso Campanella*, Rome

J. A. Fishman (1965) 'Who speaks What Language to Whom and When'; rpr. in Pride and Holmes (1972), ch. 1.

J. A. Fishman (1972) *Language in Sociocultural Change*, Stanford

P. Flaherty (1987) 'The Politics of Linguistic Uniformity during the French Revolution', *Historical Reflections* 14

C. P. Flynn (1977) *Insult and Society*, Port Washington

U. Foglietta (1574) *De ratione scribendae historiae*, Rome

G. F. Folena (1964) 'La cultura volgare e l'umanesimo cavalleresco', in *Umanesimo europeo ed umanesimo veneziano*, ed. V. Branca, Florence, 141–57

G. F. Folena (1968–70) 'Introduzione al veneziano "de là da mar"', *Bollettino dell'Atlante Linguistico Mediterraneo* 10–12, 331–76

G. F. Folena (1983) *L'italiano in Europa*, Turin

L. Formigari, ed. (1984) *Teorie e pratiche linguistiche nell'Italia del '700*, Bologna

[J. Forrester] (1734) *The Polite Philosopher*, London

C. Forstner (1626) *Notae*; 2nd edn. Leiden 1650

M. Foucault (1961) *Madness and Civilization*, abr. English trans. London 1967

M. Foucault (1975) *Discipline and Punish*, English trans. Harmondsworth 1979

154     BIBLIOGRAPHY

M. Foucault (1984) *The Use of Pleasure*, English trans. Harmondsworth 1986

C. O. Frake (1972) 'How to Ask for a Drink in Subanun'; rpr. in Giglioli, ch. 5

S. Freud (1930) *Civilisation and its Discontents*, English trans. London 1930

P. Friedrich (1966) 'Social Context and Semantic Feature: the Russian Pronominal Usage'; rpr. in Gumperz and Hymes (1972), 272–300

J. Frykman (1990) 'What People Do but Seldom Say', *Ethnologia Scandinavica* 20, 50–62

J. Frykman and O. Löfgren (1987) *Culture Builders*, New Brunswick

M. Fulbrook (1983) *Piety and Politics*, Cambridge

M. Fumaroli (1980) *L'âge de l'éloquence*, Geneva

F. Furet (1978) *Interpreting the French Revolution*, English trans. Cambridge 1981

F. J. Furnivall, ed. (1868a) *The Babees Book*, London

F. J. Furnivall, ed. (1868b) *Caxton's Book of Courtesye*, London

F. J. Furnivall, ed. (1890) *Shakespeare's England*, London

J. Fuster (1968) 'La llengua dels moriscos', in Fuster, *Llengua, literatura, història*, Barcelona, 391–430

H.-G. Gadamer (1965) *Truth and Method*, English trans. London 1975

A. L. de Gaetano (1976) *G. B. Gelli and the Florentine Academy: the Rebellion against Latin*, Florence

P. Gardy (1978) *Langue et société en Provence*, Paris

D. Garrioch (1987) 'Verbal Insults in Eighteenth-Century Paris', in Burke and Porter, ch. 5

C. Geertz (1960) 'Linguistic Etiquette'; rpr. in Pride and Holmes (1972), ch. 11

C. Geertz (1983) *Local Knowledge*, New York

P. F. Gehl (1987) 'Varieties of Monastic Silence', *Viator* 18, 125–60

G. B. Gelli (1967) *Dialoghi*, ed. R. Tissoni, Bari

Aulus Gellius (1927) *Noctes Atticae*, ed. J. C. Rolfe, 3 vols, Cambridge Mass.

E. Gellner (1983) *Nations and Nationalism*, London

A. Genovesi (1775) *Lettere familiari*, 2 vols, Venice

P. Gerbenzon (1987) 'Gaf J. C. Naber werkelijk tot 1911 college in het Latijn?', *Legal History Review* 55, 387–91

A. Gerber, ed. (1903) *Lexicon Taciteum*, Leipzig

J. Gessinger (1980) *Sprache und Bürgertum*, Stuttgart

G. G. Giglioli, ed. (1972) *Language and Social Context*, Harmondsworth

F. Gilbert (1954) 'The Concept of Nationalism in Machiavelli's Prince', *Studies in the Renaissance* 1, 38–48

F. Gilbert (1965) *Machiavelli and Guicciardini*, Princeton

M. Gilsenan (1976) 'Lying, Honour and Contradiction', in *Transaction and Meaning*, ed. B. Kapferer, Philadelphia, 191–214

C. Ginzburg (1970) *Il nicodemismo: simulazione e dissimulazione religiosa nell'Europa del '500*, Turin

C. Ginzburg (1976) *Cheese and Worms*, English trans. London 1980

A. Giuffredi (1896) *Avvertimenti christiani*, ed. L. Natali, Palermo

P. Giustinelli (1609) *Antidoto contra le cattive conversazioni*, Rome

L. Glass (1991) *Confident Conversation: How to Talk in Any Business or Social Situation*, London

E. Goffman (1961) *Encounters*; 2nd edn., London 1972

E. Goffman (1981) *Forms of Talk*, Oxford

K.-H. Göttert (1987) 'Legitimation für das Kompliment', *Deutsche Vierteljahrschrift für Literaturwissenschaft und Geistesgeschichte* 61, 189–205

H. Goldblatt (1984) 'The Language Question and the Emergence of Slavic National Languages', in Scaglione (1984b), 119–73

J. Goldfriedrich (1908) *Geschichte des deutschen Buchhandels*, Leipzig

P. Goodrich (1986) *Reading the Law*, Oxford

J. Goody (1977) *The Domestication of the Savage Mind*, Cambridge

B. Gracián (1646) 'El discreto'; rpr. in Gracián, *Obras*, ed. M. Batllori, Madrid 1969, 305–65

A. Grafton and L. Jardine (1986) *From Humanism to the Humanities*, London

W. L. Grant (1954) 'European Vernacular Works in Latin Translation', *Studies in the Renaissance* 1, 120–56

A. S. Gratwick (1982) 'Latinitas Britannica', in *Latin and the Vernacular Languages in Early Medieval Britain*, ed. N. Brooks, Leicester, 1–79

A. Graziano (1984) 'Uso e diffusione dell'inglese', in Formigari, 373–94

V. H. H. Green (1979) *The Commonwealth of Lincoln College*, Oxford

S. Greenblatt (1980) *Renaissance Self-Fashioning*, Chicago

S. Greenblatt (1991) 'Kidnapping Language', in Greenblatt, *Marvelous Possessions*, Oxford, 86–118

T. M. Greene (1983) '*Il Cortegiano* and the Choice of a Game', in *Castiglione*, ed. R. W. Hanning and D. Rosand, New Haven, 1–16

F. de Grenaille (1642) *L'honnête garçon*, Paris

P. Grendler (1984) 'The Schools of Christian Doctrine in Sixteenth-Century Italy', *Church History* 53, 319–31

G. Gresslinger (1660) *Ethica complementaria*, place unknown

H. P. Grice (1975) 'The Logic of Conversation', in *Speech Acts*, ed. P. Cole and J. L. Morgan, New York, 41–58

R. D. Grillo (1989a) *Dominant Languages: Language and Hierarchy in Britain and France*, Cambridge

R. D. Grillo (1989b) 'Anthropology, Language, Politics', in *Social Anthropology and the Politics of Language*, ed. R. D. Grillo, London, 1–24

H. Grotius (1657) *Annales et Historiae de rebus belgicis*, Amsterdam

H. Grünert (1974) *Sprache und Politik*, Berlin

S. Guazzo (1574) *La civil conversazione*; rev. edn. Venice 1590

R. Guha (1983) *Elementary Aspects of Peasant Insurgency in Colonial India*, New Delhi

J. Guidi (1980) 'De l'amour courtois à l'amour sacré: la condition de la femme dans l'oeuvre de B. Castiglione', *Centre de Recherches sur la Renaissance* 8, 9–80

J. Guidi (1983) 'Reformulations de l'idéologie aristocratique au 16e siècle', *Centre de Recherches sur la Renaissance* 11, 121–84

H.-U. Gumbrecht (1978) *Funktionen parlamentarischer Rhetorik in der französischen Revolution*, Munich

J. Gumperz (1972) 'The Speech Community', in Giglioli, ch. 10

J. Gumperz (1982a) *Discourse Strategies*, Cambridge

J. Gumperz (1982b) *Language and Social Identity*, Cambridge

J. Gumperz and D. Hymes, eds (1972) *Directions in Sociolinguistics*, New York

J. Habermas (1970) *On the Logic of the Social Sciences*, English trans. Cambridge 1989

R. A. Hall (1942) *The Italian 'Questione della Lingua'*, Chapel Hill

R. A. Hall (1960) 'Thorstein Veblen and Linguistic Theory', *American Speech* 35, 124–30

R. A. Hall (1974) *External History of the Romance Languages*, Chapel Hill

M. A. K. Halliday (1978) *Language as Social Semiotic*, London

S. Harding (1975) 'Women and Words in a Spanish Village', in *Toward an Anthropology of Women*, ed. R. R. Reiter, New York and London, 283–308

G. Harsdörffer (1641–9) *Frauernzimmers Gesprächspiele*, Nuremberg

R. Hatton (1978) *George I*, London

S. B. Heath (1972) *Telling Tongues: Language Policy in Mexico, Colony to Nation*, New York and London

S. B. Heath and R. Laprade (1982) 'Castilian Colonization and Indigenous Languages: the Cases of Quechua and Aymara', in Cooper 118–43

C. Henn-Schmölder (1975) 'Ars conversationis', *Arcadia* 10, 16–73

G. Hess (1971) *Deutsch-Lateinisch Narrenzunft*, Munich

P. Higonnet (1980) 'The Politics of Linguistic Terrorism', *Social History* 5, 41–69

C. Hill (1965) *Intellectual Origins of the English Revolution*, Oxford

C. Hill (1972) *The World Turned Upside Down: Radical Ideas during the English Revolution*; 2nd edn. Harmondsworth 1975

M. Hinz (1992) *Rhetorische Strategien des Hoffmannes*, Stuttgart

E. J. Hobsbawm (1990) *Nations and Nationalism since 1780*, Cambridge

E. J. Hobsbawm and T. Ranger, eds (1983), *The Invention of Tradition*, Cambridge

L. Holberg (1970) *Memoirs*, English trans. Leiden

G. Holmes (1986) *Florence, Rome and the Origins of the Renaissance*, Oxford

A. Hudson (1981) 'A Lollard Sect Vocabulary'; rpr. in Hudson, *Lollards and their Books*, London 1985, 165–80

G. Hughes (1991) *Swearing: a Social History of Foul Language, Oaths and Profanity in English*, Oxford

J. Huizinga (1924) *Erasmus of Rotterdam*, English trans. London 1952

L. Hunt (1984) *Politics, Culture and Class in the French Revolution*, Berkeley

J. Hunter (1988) 'Language reform in Meiji Japan: the Views of Maejima Hisoka', in *Themes and Theories in Japanese History*, ed. S. Henny and J.-P. Lehman, London, 101–20

D. Hymes (1964) 'Towards Ethnographies of Communication'; rpr. in Giglioli (1972), 21–41

D. Hymes (1974) 'Ways of Speaking', in Bauman and Sherzer, ch. 21

Ignatius (1963) *Obras completas de I. de Loyola*, ed. I. Iparraguirre, Madrid

J. Ijsewijn (1977) *Companion to Neolatin Studies*; 2nd edn. Leuven 1990

J. Ijsewijn (1987) 'Neolatin: a Historical Survey', *Helios* 14, 93–107

V. Ilardi (1956) 'Italianità among some Italian Intellectuals in the Early Sixteenth Century', *Traditio* 12, 339–67

I. Illich (1983) *Gender*, London

S. Infessura (1890) *Diario*, ed. O. Tommasini, Rome

C. Irson (1662) *Nouvelle méthode pour apprendre la langue française*; rpr. Geneva 1973

J. Irvine (1974) 'Strategies of Status Manipulation in the Wolof Greeting', in Bauman and Sherzer, ch. 8

F.-A. Isambert (1827–33) *Recueil général des anciennes lois françaises*, 29 vols, Paris

K. Jackson (1948) 'On the Vulgar Latin of Roman Britain', *Medieval Studies in Honour of J. D. M. Ford*, ed. U. T. Holmes and A. J. Denomy, Cambridge, Mass., 83–106

C. S. Jaeger (1985) *The Origins of Courtliness*, Philadelphia

M. Jay (1982) 'Should Intellectual History take a Linguistic Turn?', in *Modern European Intellectual History*, ed. D. LaCapra and S. L. Kaplan, Ithaca and London, 86–110

M. Jeanneret (1987) *A Feast of Words: Banquets and Table Talk in the Renaissance*, English trans. Chicago 1991

O. Jespersen (1905) *Growth and Structure of the English Language*, Leipzig

F. R. Johnson (1944) 'Latin versus English: the Sixteenth-Century Debate over Scientific Terminology', *Studies in Philology* 41, 109–35

I. G. Jones (1980) 'Language and Community in Nineteenth-Century Wales', in *A People and a Proletariat*, ed. D. Smith, 47–71

R. F. Jones (1953) *The Triumph of the English Language*, Stanford

B. Jonson (1953) *Timber*, New York

P. Joutard (1977) *La légende des Camisards*, Paris

P. Joyce (1991) 'The People's English: Language and Class in England, *c*.1840–1920', in Burke and Porter, 154–90

I. Kajanto (1979) 'The Position of Latin in Eighteenth-Century Finland', *Acta Conventus Neo-Latini Amstelodamensis*, ed. P. Tuynman et al., Munich, 93–106

K. H. Karpat (1984) 'A Language in Search of a Nation: Turkish in the Nation-State', in Scaglione (1984b), 175–208

L. C. Heating (1941) *Studies on the Literary Salon in France, 1550–1615*, Cambridge, Mass.

D. Kent (1978) *The Rise of the Medici*, Oxford

D. Kent and F. W. Kent (1982) *Neighbours and Neighbourhood in Renaissance Florence*, Locust Valley

V. Kiernan (1991) 'Languages and Conquerors', in Burke and Porter, 191–210

D. Kimpel, ed. (1985) *Mehrsprachigkeit in der deutschen Aufklärung*, Hamburg

H. W. Klein (1957) *Latein und volgare in Italien*, Munich

A. Knigge (1788) *Über den Umgang mit Menschen*, 3rd edn., Frankfurt and Leipzig

J. Knowlson (1975) *Universal Language Schemes in England and France 1600–1800*, Toronto

R. Koselleck (1979) *Futures Past*, English trans. Cambridge, Mass. 1985, 73–91.

W. Kühlmann (1985) 'Apologie und Kritik des Lateins im Schrifttum des deutschen Späthumanismus', in Schoeck, 356–76

J. Kühn (1975) *Gescheiterte Sprachkritik*, Berlin

W. Labov (1972a) *Sociolinguistic Patterns*, Philadelphia

W. Labov (1972b) *Language in the Inner City*, Philadelphia

J. La Bruyère (1688) *Les caractères*, Paris

R. T. Lakoff (1975) *Language and Women's Place*, New York

R. T. Lakoff (1990) *Talking Power*, New York

Lambert, Marquise de (1843) *Oeuvres morales*, Paris

R. Landes (1947) *City of Women*, New York

F. La Mothe Le Vayer (1643–4) *Opuscules*, 2 vols, Paris

A. Langer (1954) *Der Wortschatz des Deutschen Pietismus*, Tübingen

La Rochefoucauld, Duc de (1946) *Maximes*, ed. F. C. Green, Cambridge

La Rochefoucauld, Duc de (1950) *Oeuvres*, ed. L. Martin-Chauffier, Paris

J.-Y. Lartichaux (1977) 'Linguistic Politics during the French Revolution', *Diogenes* 97, 65–84

J.-B. de La Salle (1695) *Les règles de la bienséance*; rpr. Rouen 1764

R. Lass, ed. (1969) *Approaches to English Historical Linguistics*, New York

A. La Vopa (1988) *Grace, Talent and Merit: Poor Students, Clerical Careers and Professional Ideology in Eighteenth-Century Germany*, Cambridge

L. Lazzerini (1978) 'Introduzione', to A. Calmo, *La Spagnolas*, Milan

P. Lehmann (1929) 'Vom Leben des Lateinischen im Mittelalter'; in Lehmann, *Erforschung des Mittelalters*, Leipzig 1941

J. Lehtonen and K. Sajavaara (1985) 'The Silent Finn', in Tannen and Saville-Troika, 193–201

L. Le Laboureur (1667) *Avantages de la langue française sur la langue Latine*, Paris

H. Ormsby Lennon (1991) 'From Shibboleth to Apocalypse: Quaker Speechways during the Puritan Revolution', in Burke and Porter, 72–112

L. Lentner (1964) *Volksprache und Sakralsprache: Geschichte einer Lebensfrage bis zum Ende des Konzil von Trient*, Vienna

L. de León (1583) *La perfecta casada*, Salamanca

G. Leopardi (1824) 'Discorso sopra lo stato presente dei costumi degl'Italiani'; rpr. in Leopardi, *Opere*, vol. 1, ed. S. Solmi, Milan and Naples 1956, 844–77

R. B. Le Page and A. Tabouret-Keller (1985) *Acts of Identity*, Cambridge

E. Le Roy Ladurie (1966) *The Peasants of Languedoc*, English trans. Urbana 1974

E. Le Roy Ladurie (1975) *Montaillou*, English trans. Harmondsworth

K. Liebreich (1985–6) 'Piarist Education in the 17th Century', *Studi secenteschi* 26, 225–78, and 27, 57–89

J. L. Lievsay (1940) 'Notes on the *Art of Conversation* (1738)', *Italica* 17, 58–63

J. L. Lievsay (1961) *Stefano Guazzo and the English Renaissance*, Chapel Hill

John Locke (1693) *Some Thoughts concerning Education*; ed. J. Yolton, Oxford 1989

J. Locke (1953) *Travels in France*, ed. J. Lough, Cambridge

W. B. Lockwood (1965) *An Informal History of the German Language*, London

O. Löfgren (1987) 'Deconstructing Swedishness', in *Anthropology at Home*, ed. A. Jackson, London, 74–93

G. P. Lomazzo (1627) *Rabisch dra Academigli dor Compa Zavargna*, 2nd edn., Milan

D. Lombard (1990) *Le carrefour javanais*, 3 vols, Paris

N. Loraux (1981) *The Invention of Athens*, English trans. Cambridge, Mass. 1986

G. F. Loredano (1676) *Bizzarie academiche*, Bologna

F. Lot (1931) 'A quelle époque a-t-on cessé de parler Latin?', *Bulletin du Cange* 6, 97–159

J. Lough (1984) *France Observed in the Seventeenth Century*, Stocksfield

J. B. Lynch (1966) 'Lomazzo and the Accademia della Valle di Bregno', *Art Bulletin* 48, 210–11

J. Lyons (1980) 'Pronouns of Address in *Anna Karenina*', in *Studies in Linguistics for R. Quirk*, London, 235–49

M. Lyons (1981) 'Politics and Patois: the Linguistic Policy of the French Revolution', *Australian Journal of French Studies* 264–81

S. McConnell-Ginet (1978) 'Intonation in a Man's World', *Signs* 3, 541–59

E. McCumfrey (1987) 'Silence', in *Encyclopaedia of Religion*, ed M. Eliade, New York, vol. 13, 321–4

O. MacDonagh (1983) *States of Mind: a Study of Anglo-Irish Conflict 1780–1980*, London

M. McDonald (1989) 'The Exploitation of Linguistic Mis-Match: Towards an Ethnography of Customs and Manners', in *Social Anthropology and the Politics of Language*, ed. R.D. Grillo, 90–105

C. McIntosh (1986) *Common and Courtly Language*, Philadelphia

R. Mackenney (1987) *Tradesmen and Traders*, London

I. Maclean (1977) *Woman Triumphant: Feminism in French Literature, 1610–52*, Oxford

M. McLuhan (1964) *Understanding Media*, New York

R. Macmullen (1962) 'Roman Bureaucratese', *Traditio* 18, 364–78

M. Magendie (1925) *La politesse mondaine en France au 17e siècle*, Paris

B. Magne (1976) *Crise de la littérature française*, Paris

E. Magne (1912) *Voiture et les années de gloire de l'hôtel de Rambouillet*, Paris

Y. Malkiel (1976) 'Changes in the European Languages under a New Set of Sociolinguistic Circumstances', rpr. in Chiappelli (1985), 581–93

Y. Malkiel (1984) 'A Linguist's View of the Standardization of a Dialect', in Scaglione (1984b), 51–73

M. Manitius (1911–31) *Geschichte der lateinischen Literatur des Mittelalters*, 3 vols, Munich

Marcabru (1909) *Poésies complètes*, ed. J. M. L. Dejeanne, Toulouse

E. D. Marcu (1976) *Sixteenth-Century Nationalism*, New York

C. J. Margerison (1987) *If Only I Had Said*, London

C. Markham, ed. (1895) *Narratives*, London

Z. R. W. M. von Martels (1989) *Augerius Gislenius Busbequius*, Groningen

H.-J. Martin (1969) *Livre, pouvoirs et société à Paris*, The Hague

J. Martin (1987) 'A Journeyman's Feast of Fools', *Journal of Medieval and Renaissance Studies* 17, 149–74

E. Masini (1665) *Sacro Arsenale*, Bologna

W. Matthews (1936–7) 'Polite Speech in the Eighteenth Century', *English* 1, 493–511

T. de Mauro (1963) *Storia linguistica dell'Italia unita*; 2nd edn. Rome and Bari, 1976

F. Mauthner (1902–3) *Beiträge zu einer Kritik der Sprache*, 3 vols, Stuttgart

A. Mazrui (1978) *The Political Sociology of the English Language*, London

J. A. Mazzeo (1962) 'St Augustine's Rhetoric of Silence', *Journal of the History of Ideas* 23, 175–96

A. Meillet (1921) *Linguistique historique et linguistique générale*, Paris

A. Meillet (1928) *Esquisse d'une histoire de la langue latin*, Paris

G. Mensching (1926) *Das heilige Schweigen*, Giessen

Méré, Chevalier de (1677) 'De la conversation'; rpr. in his *Discours*, ed. C.-H. Boudhors, Paris 1930, 99–132

B. Migliorini (1960) *Storia della lingua italiana*, Milan

G. Milanesi, ed. (1901) *Nuovi documenti per la storia dell'arte toscana*, Florence

R. A. Miller (1971) 'Levels of Speech and the Japanese Linguistic Response to Modernization', in *Tradition and Modernization*, ed. D. Shively, Berkeley and Los Angeles

N. Mitford, ed. (1956) *Noblesse oblige*, London

G. B. Mittarelli, ed. (1755–73), *Annales Camaldulenses*, 9 vols, Venice

C. Mohrmann (1932) *Die altchristliche Sondersprache in den Sermones des hl. Augustin*, Nijmegen

C. Mohrmann (1957) *Liturgical Latin*, English trans. London 1959

C. Mohrmann (1958–61) *Études sur le latin des chrétiens*, 2 vols, Rome

Molière (1962) *Théâtre*, Paris

G. Mongrédien (1947) *La vie littéraire au 17e siècle*, Paris

M. de Montaigne (1588) *Essais*; ed. M. Rat, 3 vols, Paris 1955

M. de Montaigne (1992) *Journal*, ed. F. Rigolot, Paris

P. Moogk (1979) 'Thieving Buggers and Stupid Sluts: Insults and Popular Culture in New France', *William and Mary Quarterly* 36, 523–47

Morellet, Abbé (1812) 'De la conversation'; rpr. in his *Mélanges de litterature et de philosophie*, 4 vols, Paris 1818, vol. 4, 71–130

G. di P. Morelli (1956) *Ricordi*, ed. V. Branca, Florence

S. E. Morison (1936) *Harvard College in the Seventeenth Century*, Cambridge Mass.

T. Morison (1927) 'Un français à la cour du grand Mogol', *Revue historique* 156, 83–97

I. Morris (1964) *The World of the Shining Prince*, London

J.-B. Morvan de Bellegarde (1697) *Modèles de conversations pour les personnes polies*, Paris

J.-B. Morvan de Bellegarde (1703) *Reflexions sur la politesse*, 3rd edn, Paris

R. Muchembled (1978) *Popular Culture and Elite Culture in*

*Early Modern France*, English trans. Baton Rouge 1985

R. Muchembled (1989) *La violence au village*, Tournhout

B. L. de Muralt (1728) *Lettres sur les anglois et les françois*; ed. C. Gould, Paris 1933

G. Muzio (1572) *Discorso per la unione d'Italia*, Rome

S. Nagel and S. Vecchi (1984) 'Il bambino, la parola, il silenzio nella cultura medievale', *Quaderni Storici* 19, 719–63

J. R. Naiden (1952) 'Newton Demands the Latin Muse', *Symposium* 111–20

C. Newman (1957) *The Evolution of Medical Education in the Nineteenth Century*, London

O. Niccoli (1979) *I sacerdoti i guerrieri i contadini: storia di un'immagine della società*, Turin

R. Nigro (1990) 'Gli atti di parola nella "Civil conversatione"', in Patrizi, 95–120

T. Nipperdey (1983) 'In Search of Identity: Romantic Nationalism, its Intellectual Political and Social Background', in *In Search of Identity*, ed. J. C. Eade, Canberra, 1–15

G. da Nono (1934–9) 'Visio Egidii Regis Pataviae', ed. G. Fabris, *Bollettino del Civico Museo di Padova* 10–11, 1–20

P. Nora, ed. (1984–6), *Les lieux de mémoire*, 4 vols, Paris

D. Norberg (1975–6) 'Latin scolaire et latin vivant', *Bulletin du Cange* 40, 51–64

E. Norden (1898) *Die Antike Kunstprosa*; 5th edn, Stuttgart 1958

W. Notestein et al., eds (1935), *Commons Debates 1621*, 7 vols, New Haven

P. H. Nurse (1968) 'Erasme et des Périers', *Bibliothèque d'Humanisme et Renaissance* 30, 53–64

E. Österberg (1991) 'Strategies of Silence: Milieu and Mentality in the Icelandic Sagas', in Österberg, *Mentalities and Other Realities*, Lund and Bromley, 9–30

G. Oestreich (1982) *Neostoicism and the Early Modern State*, Cambridge

C. Ogier (1656) *Ephemerides*, Paris

J. C. Olin, ed. (1965) *Christian Humanism and the Reformation*, New York

W. J. Ong (1958) *Ramus: Method and the Decay of Dialogue*, Cambridge, Mass.

W. J. Ong (1959) 'Latin Language Study as a Renaissance Puberty

Rite', *Studies in Philology* 56, 103–24

M. Opitz (1617) *Aristarchus, sive de contemptu linguae teutonicae*; rpr. Leipzig 1888

A. Orero, ed. (1595) *Rime diverse in lingua Genovese*, Pavia

P. Ortigue de Vaumorière (1688) *L'art de plaire dans la conversation*, Paris

C. Ossola (1983) 'L'homme accomplie: la civilisation des cours comme art de la conversation'; rpr. in Ossola, *Dal Cortegiano all Uomo di Mondo*, Turin 1987, 131–9

*Oxford English Dictionary* (1989), 2nd edn, ed. J. A. Simpson and E. S. C. Weiner, 20 vols, Oxford

I. Paccagnella (1984) *Il fasto delle lingue*, Rome

I. Paccagnella (1987) 'Plurilinguismo letterario', *Letteratura Italiana*, vol. 2, ed. A. Asor Rosa, 2, Turin, 103–67

A. Pagden, ed. (1987) *The Languages of Political Theory in Early Modern Europe*, Cambridge

L. Palmireno (1577) *El estudoso cortesano*; 2nd edn Alcalà 1587

U. E. Paoli (1959) *Il latino maccheronico*, Florence

H. Paolucci (1984) 'Italian and English: Models for the Modern Vernacular Literatures of India', in Scaglione (1984b), 209–31

H. Parret and J. Verschueren, eds (1992) (on) *Searle on Conversation*, Amsterdam and Philadelphia

J. Pasek (1929) *Memoirs of the Polish Baroque*, English trans. Berkeley 1976

E. Pasquier (1566) *Recherches de la France*, Paris

G. Patrizi, ed. (1990) *Stefano Guazzo e la civil conversatione*, Rome

R. Payne (1981) 'When Saying is Doing', in *Politically Speaking: Cross-Cultural Studies of Rhetoric*, ed. Payne, St John's, 9–23

A. Pease and A. Garner (1985) *Talk Language*; rpr. London 1989

A. Petrie (1720) 'Rules of Good Deportment'; rpr. in Petrie, *Works*, Edinburgh 1877, 5–136

A. Petrucci (1982) *Scrittura e popolo nella Roma barocca*, Rome

K. C. Phillipps (1984) *Language and Class in Victorian England*, London

A. Piccolomini (1539) *Raffaella*; rpr. Milano 1969

J. Pina Cabral (1987) 'Paved Roads and Enchanted Mooresses', *Man* 22, 715–35

B. Pino (1604) *Del Galantuomo*, Venice

H. L. Piozzi (1974) *Anecdotes of the Late Samuel Johnson*, Oxford

M. Plaisance (1973) 'La transformation de l'académie des Humidi en Académie Florentine', in *Les écrivains et le pouvoir*, ed. A. Rochon, Paris, 361–433

Plutarch (1927–69) *Moralia*, 16 vols, Cambridge, Mass.

J. G. A. Pocock (1972) *Politics, Language and Time*, London

G. Politiano (1547) *Del parlare e del tacere*, Milan

R. Porter (1987) 'The Language of Quackery in England, 1660–1800', in Burke and Porter, 73–103

R. Porter (1991) 'Expressing Yourself Ill: the Language of Sickness in Georgian England', in Burke and Porter, 276–99

E. Post (1922) *Etiquette in Society, in Business, in Politics and at Home*, New York and London

M. L. Pratt (1987) 'Linguistic Utopias', in *The Linguistics of Writing*, ed. N. Fabb et al., Manchester, 48–66

J. B. Pride and J. Holmes, eds (1972) *Sociolinguistics*, Harmondsworth

M. Puppo, ed. (1957) *Discussioni linguistiche del '700*, Turin

G. Puttenham (1589) *The Art of English Poesie*, London

A. Quondam (1982) 'L'Accademia', *Letteratura italiana*, vol. 1, ed. A. Asor Rosa, Turin, 823–98

A. Quondam (1983) 'La letteratura in tipografia', in *Letteratura Italiana*, vol. 2, ed. A. Asor Rosa, Turin, 555–686

G. Rajberti (1850–1) *L'arte di convitare*, Milan

E. S. Ramage (1973) *Urbanitas*, Norman

W. S. Ramson (1970) 'Nineteenth-Century Australian English', in Ramson, *English Transported*, Canberra, 32–48

O. Ranum (1980) *Artisans of Glory: Writers and Historical Thought in Seventeenth-Century France*, Chapel Hill

E. du Refuge (1617) *Traité de la Cour*, Rouen 1631

A. Renaud (1697) *Manière de parler la langue française selon ses différents styles*

B. Richardson (1987) 'Gli italiani e il toscano parlato nel '500', *Lingua Nostra* 44, 97–107

M. Richter (1975) 'A Sociolinguistic Approach to the Latin Middle Ages', in *Materials and Methods of Ecclesiastical History*, ed. D. Baker, Oxford, 69–82

M. Richter (1979) *Sprache und Gesellschaft im Mittelalter*, Stuttgart

M. Richter (1983) 'A quelle époque a-t-on cessé de parler latin en Gaule?', *Annales E.S.C.* 38, 439–48

I. Ringhiera (1551) *Cento giuochi liberali*, Bologna

T. Rinuccini (1863) *Usanze fiorentine del secolo* XVII, Florence

S. Rizzo (1986) 'Il latino nell'umanesimo', *Letteratura italiana*, vol. 5, ed. A. Asor Rosa, Turin, 379–410

R. Robin (1973) *Histoire et linguistique*, Paris

J. H. Rodrigues (1985) 'The Victory of the Portuguese Language in Colonical Brazil', in *Empire in Transition*, ed. A. Hower and R. Preto-Rodas, Gainesville, 22–30

D. de Rosa (1980) *Coluccio Salutati*, Florence

H. Rosen (1972) *Language and Class*, Bristol

L. Rosen (1984) *Bargaining for Reality*, Cambridge

A. Rosenblat (1977) 'La hispanización de América. El castellano y las lenguas indígenas desde 1492', in Rosenblat, *Los conquistadores y su lengua*, Caracas, 91–136

A. S. C. Ross (1954) 'Linguistic Class-Indicators in Present-Day English', *Neuphilologische Mitteilungen* 55, 20–56

C. Roubert (1972) 'Un jeu de société au Grand Siècle', *17e Siècle* 97, 85–102

L. von Rozmital (1957) *Travels*, ed. M. Letts, Cambridge

F. des Rues (1603) *Les marguerites françoises*, Lyon

T. Rymer, ed. (1704–32) *Foedera*, 20 vols, London

'O. Sabertash' (1842) *The Art of Conversation*, London

J. Saenz, ed. (1755) *Collectio Maxima Conciliorum Omnium Hispaniae*, Rome

T. Sagittarius (1603) *De conversatione civili*; rpr. Leiden 1650

L. Sainéan (1907) *L'Argot ancien*, Paris

St-Simon, Duc de (1983–8) *Mémoires*, ed. Y. Coirault, 8 vols, Paris

V. Salmon (1967) 'Elizabethan Colloquial English', *Leeds Studies in English*

W. Samarin (1972) *Tongues of Men and Angels*, New York

M. Sanudo (1879–1903) *Diarii*, 58 vols, Venice

M. Sanudo (1980) *La città di Venetia*, ed. A. Caracciolo Aricò, Milan

[G. Savile] (1688) *The Lady's New-Year Gift, or Advice to a Daughter*, London

M. Saville-Troike (1982) *The Ethnography of Communication*, Oxford

M. Saville-Troika (1985) 'The Place of Silence in an Integrated Theory of Communication', in Tannen and Saville-Troika, 3–18

F. Saxl (1957) 'Jacopo Bellini and Mantegna as Antiquarians', in Saxl, *Lectures*, 2 vols, London, vol. 1, 150–60

A. Scaglione (1984a) 'The Rise of National Languages: East and West', in Scaglione (1984b), 9–49

A. Scaglione, ed. (1984b) *The Emergence of National Languages*, Ravenna

S. Schama (1987) *The Embarrassment of Riches*, London

E. A. Schegloff (1988) 'Goffman and the Analysis of Conversation', in *Erving Goffman*, ed. P. Drew and A. Wootton, Cambridge, 89–139

A. Schiaffini (1937) 'Aspetti della crisi linguistica italiana del '700'; rpr. in Schiaffini, *Italiano antico e moderno*, Milan and Naples 1975, 129–65

H. Schmidt (1950) *Liturgie et langue vulgaire*, Rome

R. J. Schoeck, ed. (1985) *Acta Conventus Neolatini Bononiensis*, Binghamton

J. Schrijnen (1932) *Charakteristik des Altchristlichen Latein*, Nijmegen

J. Schrijnen (1939) 'Le Latin chrétien devenu langue commune', in Schrijnen, *Collectanea*, Nijmegen, 335–56

J. C. Scott (1976) *The Moral Economy of the Peasant*, New Haven

M. de Scudéry (1680) *Conversations sur divers sujets*, Paris

J. U. Sebeok and T. A. Sebeok, eds (1987) *Monastic Sign Language*, Berlin

F. Seager (1577) *The School of Virtue*; rpr. in Furnivall (1868a)

J. R. Searle (1992) 'Conversation', in Parret and Verschueren, 7–30

J. Seigel (1966) 'Civic Humanism or Ciceronian Rhetoric?', *Past and Present* 34, 3–48

W. S. Sewell (1980) *The Language of Labor*, Cambridge

D. Sheerin (1987) 'In media latinitate', *Helios* 14, 51–67

P. Sidney (1973) *Miscellaneous Prose*, Oxford

J. Siegel (1986) *Solo in the New Order*, Princeton

D. Simpson (1986) *The Politics of American English 1776–1850*, New York

P. Skippon (1732) 'An Account of a Journey', in *A Collection of Voyages*, ed. A. and J. Churchill, 6 vols, London, vol. 6

M. M. Slaughter (1982) *Universal Languages and Scientific Taxonomy in the Seventeenth Century*, Cambridge

A. D. Smith (1986) *The Ethnic Origins of Nations*, London

O. Smith (1984) *The Politics of Language 1791–1819*, Oxford

C. A. Sneyd, ed. (1843) *A Relation of the Island of England*, London

B. T. Sozzi (1955) *Aspetti e momenti della questione linguistica*, Padua

H. Spencer (1861) *Essays on Education*; rpr. London 1911

D. Spender (1980) *Man-Made Language*, London

A. Spinola (1981) *Scritti scelti*, ed. C. Bitossi, Genoa

L. Spitzer (1955) 'The Problem of Latin Renaissance Poetry', rpr. in his *Romanische Literaturstudien*, Tübingen 1959, 923–44

G. Stedman Jones (1983) *Languages of Class*, Cambridge

G. Steiner (1966) 'Silence and the Poet'; rpr. in Steiner, *Language and Silence*, Harmondsworth 1969, 57–76

J. Stevens (1961) *Music and Poetry in the Early Tudor Court*, London

B. Stolt (1964) *Die Sprachmischung in Luthers Tischreden*, Stockholm

L. Stone (1977) *Family, Sex and Marriage in England*, London

L. Stone (1992) *Road to Divorce: England 1530–1987*, Oxford

J. Stow (1601) *The Annales of England*, London

B. M. H. Strang (1970) *A History of English*, London

T. B. Strong (1984) 'Language and Nihilism: Nietzsche's Critique of Epistemology', rpr. in *Language and Politics*, ed. M. Shapiro, Oxford, ch. 6

C. Strosetzki (1978) *Konversation: ein Kapitel gesellschaftlicher und literarischer Pragmatik im Frankreich des 17. Jahrhunderts*, Frankfurt

N. S. Struever (1974) 'The Study of Language and the Study of History', *Journal of Interdisciplinary History* 4, 401–16

A. Stussi (1972) 'Lingua, dialetto e letteratura', *Storia d'Italia*, ed. R. Romano and C. Vivanti, Turin, vol. 1, 680–728

J. Sutherland, ed. (1953) *The Oxford Book of English Talk*, Oxford

K. W. Swart (1978) *William the Silent and the Revolt of the Netherlands*, London

D. M. Swetschinski (1982) 'The Portuguese Jews of Amsterdam', in *Essays on Modern Jewish History*, ed. F. Malino and P. C. Albert, Toronto, 56–80

J. Swift (1939–68) *Prose Works*, ed. H. Davis et al., Oxford

L. Tacchella (1966) *La riforma tridentina nella diocesi di Tortona*, Genoa

M. Tafuri, ed. (1984) *Renovatio Urbis*, Turin

C. Tagliareni (1954) *Opera manuscritta del marchese G. B. Del Tufo*, Naples

S. J. Tambiah (1968) 'The Magical Power of Words', rpr. in Tambiah, *Culture, Thought and Social Action*, Cambridge, Mass, 1985, 17–59

D. Tannen (1984) *Conversational Style*, Norwood N.J.

D. Tannen (1986) *That's Not What I Meant!*, London

D. Tannen (1990) 'Silence as Conflict Management in Fiction and Drama', in *Conflict Talk*, ed. A. D. Grimshaw, Cambridge, 260–79

D. Tannen and M. Saville-Troika, eds (1985) *Perspectives on Silence*, Norwood N.J.

M. Tavoni (1984) *Latino, grammatica, volgare*, Padua

M. Tavoni (1985) 'Sulla difesa del Latino nel '500', in *Renaissance Studies in Honor of C. H. Smyth*, Florence, 493–505

T. J. Taylor and D. Cameron (1987) *Analysing Conversation*, Oxford

W. Thomas (1549) *The History of Italy*; ed. G. B. Parkes, Ithaca 1963

E. P. Thompson (1975) 'The Crime of Anonymity', in *Albion's Fatal Tree*, ed. D. Hay et al., London, ch. 2

J. A. de Thou (1838) *Mémoires*, Paris

M. Timotei (1614) *Il Cortegiano*, Rome

R. P. Toby (1986) 'Carnival of the Aliens: Korean Embassies in Edo-Period Art and Popular Culture', *Monumenta Nipponica* 41, 415–56

J. R. R. Tolkien and E. V. Gordon, eds (1925) *Sir Gawain and the Green Knight*, Oxford

A. Traina (1971) *Il latino del Pascoli*, Florence

E. Travi (1984) 'Il volgare nella liturgia', in Travi *Lingua e vita nel primo '500*, Milan, 47–62

O. Treitinger (1938) *Die Oströmische Kaiser- und Reichsidee*; rpr. Darmstadt 1956

J. Trotti de la Chetardye (1683) *Instructions pour un jeune seigneur*, Paris

J. Trotti de la Chetardye (1685) *Instruction pour une jeune princesse*, Paris

B. Trotto (1578) *Dialoghi del matrimonio*, Turin

P. Trudgill (1974) *Sociolinguistics*, Harmondsworth

J. Trusler (1775) *Principles of Politeness*, London

J. Twigg (1987) *A History of Queens' College Cambridge*, Woodbridge

S. A. Tyler (1978) *The Said and the Unsaid*, New York

J. M. Valentin (1978) *Le théâtre des Jésuites dans les pays de langue allemande*, Bern

B. Varchi (1570) *L'Ercolano*, Florence

C. Vasoli (1986) 'Sperone Speroni e la nascita della coscienza nazionale come coscienza linguistica', in *Cultura e nazione in Italia e Polonia*, ed. V. Branca and S. Graciotti, Florence, 161–80

C. de Vaugelas (1647) *Remarques sur la langue française*, ed. J. Streicher, Paris 1934

Vauvenargues, Marquis de (1968) *Oeuvres*, ed. H. Bonnier, 2 vols, Paris

T. Veblen (1899) *The Theory of the Leisure Class*, New York

M. Venard (1985) 'Le visite pastorali francesi dal XVI al XVIII secolo', in *Le visite pastorali*, ed. U. Mazzone and A. Turchini, Bologna, 13–55

E. Veres, ed. (1944) *Báthory István Levelezése*, 2 vols, Kolozsvár [Cluj]

Vespasiano de Bisticci (1970–6) *Vite di uomini illustri*, 2 vols, Florence

N. Vianello (1957) 'Il Veneziano, lingua del foro veneto', *Lingua Nostra* 18, 67–73

G. B. Vico (1929) *Autobiographia e carteggio*, ed. B. Croce and F. Nicolini, Bari

M. Vidal (1992) *Watteau's Painted Conversations*, New Haven and London

P. de Vigneulles (1927–33) *Chronique*, ed. C. Bruneau, 4 vols, Metz

J.-B. Primi Visconti (1908) *Mémoires*, ed. J. Lemoine, Paris

J. A. Vissac (1862) *De la poésie latine en France au siècle de Louis XIV*, Paris

M. Vitale (1953) *La lingua volgare della cancelleria visconteo-sforzesco nel '400*, Varese and Milan

M. Vitale (1962) *La questione della lingua*; 2nd edn, Palermo 1978

K. Vossler (1913) *Frankreichs Kultur im Spiegel seiner Sprachentwicklung*, Heidelberg

K. Vossler (1924) *Sprachgemeinschaft und Interessengemeinschaft*, Munich

M. de Vries (1991) 'Twee minuten lang stilstaan bij de doden', in *Feestelijk Vernieuwing in Nederland*, ed. J. Boissevain, Amsterdam, 15–26

G. E. Waas (1941) *The Legendary Character of the Emperor Maximilian*, New York

M. L. Wagner (1920) 'Amerikanisch-Spanisch und Vulgarlatein', *Zeitschrift für Romanische Philologie* 40, 286–312

M. L. Wagner (1949) *Lingue e dialetti dell'America spagnola*, Florence

L. D. Walker (1980) 'A Note on Historical Linguistics and Marc Bloch's Comparative Method', *History and Theory* 19, 154–64

M. Wall (1969) 'The Decline of the Irish Language', in *A View of the Irish Language*, ed. B. O'Cuív, Dublin, 81–90

A. Wallenstein (1912) *Briefe*, ed. H. Hallwich, Vienna

H. Walpole (1924) *Reminiscences*, ed. P. Toynbee, Oxford

R. Wardhaugh (1985) *How Conversation Works*, Oxford

R. Wardhaugh (1987) *Languages in Competition*, Oxford

J. Wardrop (1963) *The Script of Humanism*, Oxford

G. Washington (1886) *Fifty-seven Rules of Behaviour*, ed. W. O. Stoddard, Denver

J. T. Waterman (1966) *A History of the German Language*, Cambridge

F. Watson (1915) 'Clenard as an Educational Pioneer', *Classical Review* 29, 65–8, 97–100

E. Weber (1976) *Peasants into Frenchmen*, Stanford

E. de Weihe (1615) *Aulicus politicus*, Frankfurt

H. Weinrich (1985) *Wege der Sprachkultur*, Stuttgart

D. Weinstein (1968) 'The Myth of Florence', in *Florentine Studies*, ed. N. Rubinstein, London, 15–44

R. Weissmann (1985) 'Reconstructing Renaissance Sociology', in *Persons in Groups*, ed. R. Trexler, Binghamton, 39–46

R. Weissmann (1982) *Ritual Brotherhood in Renaissance Florence*, New York

C. J. Wells (1985) *German: a Linguistic History to 1945*, Oxford

T. Westrin (1900) 'Några iakttagelser angående franskan såsom diplomatiens språk', *Historisk Tidskrift* 20, 329–40

F. Whigliam (1984) *Ambition and Privilege: The Social Tropes of Elizabethan Courtesy Theory*, Berkeley and Los Angeles

K. Whinnom (1977) 'Lingua Franca: Historical Problems', in *Pidgin and Creole Linguistics*, ed. A. Valdman, Bloomington, 295–310

W. Whiteley (1969) *Swahili: the Rise of a National Language*, Cambridge

B. Whitelocke (1855) *A Journal of the Swedish Embassy*, 2 vols, London

B. Whorf (1956) *Language, Thought and Reality*, New York

G. Williams (1992) *Sociolinguistics: a Sociological Critique*, London

J. Wilson (1989) *On the Boundaries of Conversation*, Oxford

R. Wines (1981) 'Introduction', to L. von Ranke, *The Secret of World History*, New York, 1–31

P. Wolff (1971) *Western Languages AD 100–1500*, London

G. Woodbine (1943) 'The Language of English Law', *Speculum* 18, 395–436

F. Yates (1947) *French Academies of the Sixteenth Century*, London

N. Zernov (1961) *Eastern Christendom*, London

F. Zonabend (1980) *The Enduring Memory*, English trans. Cambridge 1984

# Index